Deutsch, Mitchell F.
    Doing business with the Japanese /
Mitchell F. Deutsch. -- New York : New
American Library, [1984], c1983.
    187 p. ; 23 cm.
    "NAL books."
    Includes bibliographical references.
    ISBN 0-453-00451-2

    1. United States--Commerce--Japan.
2. Japan--Commerce--United States.
3. Corporations, American--Japan.
4. Corporations, Japanese--United
States. I. Title

13 MAR 84   10045937   OMMMxc   83-21249

DOING BUSINESS
WITH
THE JAPANESE

DOING BUSINESS
WITH
THE JAPANESE

Mitchell F. Deutsch

NAL BOOKS
NEW AMERICAN LIBRARY
TIMES MIRROR
NEW YORK AND SCARBOROUGH, ONTARIO

SIGNET, SIGNET CLASSIC, MENTOR, PLUME,
MERIDIAN and NAL BOOKS are published
in the United States by The New American Library, Inc.,
1633 Broadway, New York, New York 10019,
in Canada by The New American Library of Canada Limited,
81 Mack Avenue, Scarborough, Ontario M1L 1M8

Library of Congress Cataloging in Publication Data

Deutsch, Mitchell F.
    Doing business with the Japanese.

    1. United States—Commerce—Japan.   2. Japan—Commerce
—United States.   3. Corporation, American—Japan.
4. Corporations, Japanese—United States.   I. Title.
HF3127.D48   1984   658.1'8'0952   83-21249
ISBN 0-453-00451-2

Designed by Julian Hamer

First Printing, January, 1984

1 2 3 4 5 6 7 8 9

PRINTED IN THE UNITED STATES OF AMERICA

To my uncle, Albert Deutsch

Acknowledgments

I am humbly indebted to the nearly three hundred individuals who generously found the time (in some cases weeks) to spend discussing their experiences on doing business with the Japanese. I am particularly grateful to Jon Strom, Bob Haigh, and Harriet Russell, who were a constant source of inspiration, encouragement, and, most important, contacts.

For providing an endless source of research and reference material, thanks go to the Japan External Trade Organization, the Conference Board, the Japan Society, the U.S.-Japan Foundation, the U.S. Department of Commerce, New York State Department of Commerce, Larry Bruser at Mitsui, and the Matsushita and Sony corporations.

Deep bows go to editors Channa Taub, who had the editorial insight to recognize the importance of this project at its inception, and Dan Frank, who had the endurance to see the book through to its completion. Their painstaking efforts can't be measured.

Special thanks to my agent, friend, and prudent adviser, Richard Pine, for his relentless efforts in keeping the book afloat, and for his special ability to inspire and excite the professional in me.

I am particularly indebted to Tom Cowan, whose guiding hand in text and editorial development helped breathe life into a very cumbersome project. Without his continual professional and personal support par excellence, this book would have been near impossible.

And finally, personal thanks to Murray, Merle, and Shelley for providing a moral and emotional boost when I needed it most; to Eve for her vision, faith, and patience; and to Jeff Hollender for helping create a highly supportive work environment.

Contents

Foreword

My introduction to the Japanese was one of the more painful and awkward experiences of my professional career. During the mid-1970s I was editor of a daily newsletter called *Consumer Electronics*, based in New York City. My function was to report on new trends, industry developments, money-making ideas, and the state of the consumer electronics industry in general. The most noteworthy trend at that time was the breakneck speed with which the Japanese were making inroads into the U.S. marketplace. Each day's edition was filled with yet another Japanese "miracle" success story. These stories were developing so fast it became nearly impossible to keep abreast of them all.

Trying to get the "scoop" from Japanese business executives was no easy task. First there was the language problem; then there was their general discomfort about revealing information when talking with Americans. Finally, their simple lack of response to queries about business strategy, sales projections, and planned future company developments inevitably led one to question either the general business acumen of the Japanese or their ability to understand English. At that time, there were clearly no "money-making" answers that were fit to print. The Japanese seemed impossible, unreliable, and, frankly, quite inscrutable.

This confusion and chaos increased when I went to work for a Madison Avenue public relations firm. I was hired because of my experience with the Japanese, and was assigned to work on the accounts of two of the best known U.S. subsidiaries of Japanese companies: Sony and Canon. This time my exposure to Japanese management was far more intimate and less objective. In both cases, management was a hybrid blend of American and Japanese, with the Japanese at the helm.

Client-agency relations were invariably plagued by misunderstanding and paranoia: "Why can't those Japanese appreciate and understand the way we do things here?" "Why does it always take so long to get them to make a decision?" "We want to be frank with the Americans, but will this offend the Japanese?" These and other perfectly impossible questions constantly cropped up and the answers were equally difficult and remote. Somehow, you made it through to the next day and on to the next dilemma.

Yet I was fascinated and intrigued by the Japanese—and working with them only piqued my interest further. I became tired of extrapolating and concocting explanations for the mysteries. Abandoning the protective environment of a large Madison Avenue agency, I joined forces with Sony Consumer Products Company as national advertising manager for audio products. There I awoke to find myself immersed in the foreignness and unfamiliarity of a Japanese company, face to face with the stranger that I had never fully understood. Each day, my naiveté, my confusion, and my inefficaciousness seemed to increase tenfold. I felt like a veritable upstart, completely unequipped to do my job. I worked long hours, took Japanese lessons at the Nippon Club, asked constant questions of anyone I thought could answer them, all in an attempt to better understand the nature of the beast.

But it wasn't until I became closely associated with several Americans who had spent years working and living in Japan— Americans who spoke Japanese fluently, fully understood the Japanese mindset, and had gained the full trust and confidence of the Japanese—that I first began to realize how erroneous and distorted were my own perceptions, and how truly ineffective my actions and strategies. These associates proved to me that I had much to learn, and also that there was a bizarre sense of orderliness to the Japanese way of doing things. I was truly a stranger in a strange land.

In retrospect, I was one of the lucky few taken in from the cross-cultural maelstrom by a few compassionate Japan experts, graced by their good sense, and guided by their wise advice. But what about all the others who aren't quite so lucky? For the majority of American—and Western—businessmen, doing business with the Japanese is a haphazard, confused, and clumsy affair. Most executives and professionals have had limited exposure to the Japanese professionally or personally, and allow themselves great liberties at risk-taking —often at the expense of losing a story, a client, or even a job.

In conducting the research for this book, it became clear to me that my approach to the subject of doing business would be pragmatic. Most previous books discussing the Japanese understanding of business have been managerial and academic in approach, often written to satisfy the West's curiosity about the secrets of the "miracle." I sought the wise advice of nearly three hundred Americans and Japanese with a broad variety of experiences working with each other, both here and in Japan. Presidents and directors, managers and consultants, advertising and Wall Street executives offered their advice and experience. Many, understandably fearful of offending their colleagues or clients, requested anonymity. Others, Japanese included, were bold, surprisingly candid, and all too eager to spill their hearts out.

The result is contained in the following pages. Hopefully, my search for answers and understanding will better prepare you to do the best you possibly can—when you do business with the Japanese.

—MITCHELL F. DEUTSCH
New York City

CHAPTER 1

The Problem of Doing Business with the Japanese

THE OLD BUDWEISER sign that stood in Times Square since before Prohibition—and was once the largest outdoor advertisement in the world—is gone. A visitor to the Great White Way now stares up at Sony, Aiwa, Canon, Panasonic—all Japanese multinational powerhouses promoting the leisure-time, high-tech products that have won the allegiance of literally millions of American consumers. Since colonial times, American trade has been primarily with Western Europe. No longer. In 1977, for the first time, U.S. trade with Asia surpassed our trade volume with Europe. But trade is only one side of the business coin. The flip side is market competition. All of a sudden, the folks who brought you free enterprise found the taste of competition bitter. More disturbing, when it came to sitting down at the negotiating table with the Japanese, Americans seemed to have lost their knack for doing business. Why did our professional skills and social graces suddenly appear to desert us? Why did meetings, negotiations, and prospective deals so frequently flounder, come to a standstill, and then come to a halt? What dynamic—intercorporate? intercultural? interpersonal?—is wreaking havoc in our attempts at doing business with the Japanese?

The first step to a solution of this problem is to recognize that Western business practices are not universal. The problem is not solved by claiming that Japanese ways are illogical, irrational, as well as inscrutable. To the Japanese, their understanding of business makes perfect sense; it's ours that doesn't add up. The goals of profit and growth may be universal, but the means to attain them are not. This book will help you to recognize similarities and differences between the occidental and oriental views of business, and help you bridge the gap between them.

Business is not done according to one internationally accepted code of rules and ethics, primarily because business is a form of cultural behavior. It is inseparable from social customs, cultural prejudices and ideological assumptions.

The following quiz will help you evaluate your familiarity with Japanese business practices. In order to develop and execute the strategies and approaches that will work best for you, you have to understand what the Japanese expect, as well as what they need. Without that understanding, your transactions will remain unprofitable.

Choose the most correct answer to each question. Answers are supplied on page 9.

1. The best way to introduce yourself or your company to a Japanese company is
   a. by a personal "informal" visit.
   b. by a telephone call.
   c. through a liaison or "go-between."
   d. through a lawyer.
   e. by letter.

2. When a Japanese answers "yes" to your question, you can interpret this to signify
   a. agreement.
   b. understanding.
   c. acknowledgment that you are speaking to him.
   d. that you are being given the "run around."
   e. all of the above.

3. One of the primary characteristics of group decision-making in a Japanese company is that
   a. decisions take a long time to make, and a short time to implement.
   b. decisions are made swiftly, but executed slowly.
   c. decisions are made slowly, and executed slowly.
   d. corporate back-stabbing and face-saving prevent decisions from being reached.

4. The greatest obstacle to doing business with the Japanese successfully is
   a. the U. S. Department of Commerce.
   b. Sociocultural differences, including language.
   c. Japanese-imposed tariff and nontariff trade barriers.
   d. government interference on both sides.

5. When greeting a Japanese businessman for the first time, you should
   a. shake his hand, rave about how much you enjoy tempura shrimp, then tell him your name and company responsibility.
   b. shake his hand, present your business card, then invite him home for dinner to meet the wife and kids.
   c. shake hands, exchange business cards, be friendly, and get quickly onto a first-name basis.
   d. bow three or four times, flatter his self-esteem by appropriate comments like "How do you and your people do it!"
   e. shake hands, exchange business cards, and state how much you have been looking forward to meeting him.

6. The best way to be persuasive with the Japanese is to
   a. attempt to reason with each member of the Japanese team individually.
   b. appeal to their business savvy by pointing out long-term financial benefits.
   c. attempt to communicate a sense of openness, trustworthiness, and sincerity.
   d. pile up incontrovertible evidence in support of your point of view.

7. The extraordinary need for Japanese businessmen to save face is dictated by
   a. the fact that they are generally insecure.
   b. fear of retaliation by their superiors.
   c. preservation of group harmony.
   d. a collectively bad sense of humor.

8. The traditionally polite demeanor of Japanese business-men should never be confused with
   a. a cover-up for the disdain they feel toward foreign businessmen.
   b. a gesture of friendship.
   c. good family breeding.
   d. a tendency to be dishonest.

9. One of the best ways to impress a Japanese businessman is to
   a. act according to the Japanese code of conduct.
   b. show him your superior sense of taste in food, wine, and entertainment.
   c. learn the subtleties of bowing and wear traditional Japa-nese robes.
   d. act naturally according to your own accepted code of conduct.

10. When it comes to negotiating a business partnership, the Japanese are initially most concerned with
    a. the bottom line of a company's offer.
    b. manufacturing costs and accurate delivery dates.
    c. capturing overseas markets by illegal price-cutting.
    d. the degree of trust they intuitively feel for a prospective partner.
    e. the prospective partner's past record for garnering large shares of the market.

11. When negotiating a contract with the Japanese, you should
    a. have your lawyer do all the negotiating.
    b. impress them with your sense of urgency and impatience to consummate the deal.
    c. involve the CEO and other senior officials from the very beginning.
    d. take care to get to know your prospective partner per-sonally before commencing negotiations.

12. When you receive the silent treatment during a negotiating session, it can signify that
a. the Japanese are having difficulty understanding you.
b. the Japanese feel comfortable with you.
c. the Japanese feel uncomfortable with your line of inquiry.
d. all of the above.
e. none of the above.

13. The Japanese prefer business contracts that are
a. strict, formal, and without a "renegotiation" clause.
b. unspecific, informal, and with a "renegotiation" clause.
c. gentlemen's agreements with a tacit understanding that anything can be renegotiated.
d. none of the above.
e. both *b* and *c*.

14. Most failures of American companies to succeed in the Japanese marketplace are due to
a. unrealistic expectations.
b. tariff and nontariff barriers.
c. stiff competition from Japanese companies.
d. the inability to accept short-term losses for potential long-term profit.
e. all of the above.
f. both *a* and *d*.

15. The best way to convince a prospective Japanese business partner about the virtue and value of your products/services is to
a. tell him outright while repeatedly demonstrating their true superiority.
b. tell him nothing and let the products/services sell themselves.
c. perform comparison tests giving him hands-down proof.
d. let your sales literature do the describing and your go-between put in a good word for you.

Answers: 1: c. 2: e. 3: a. 4: b. 5: e. 6: c. 7: c. 8: b.
9: d. 10: d. 11: d. 12: d. 13: e. 14: e. 15: d.

The Information Blitz:
Media, Academia, and Capitol Hill

Understanding the Japanese is not easy. From your performance on the quiz, you have some idea of how your perceptions
of the Japanese are inaccurate or distorted. A modest score
simply indicates that you lack a basic knowledge of Japanese
customs. You probably do not speak or read Japanese. Your
Western education has conditioned you to view the world
using certain criteria by which you judge what is logical or
rational and what is not—criteria often not shared by your
Japanese counterparts.

It may come as a surprise to you to have scored low when
you may have been reading widely about the Japanese and
watching the news assiduously for information about Japanese-
American relations. In fact, this is part of the problem of
dealing with the Japanese. Too much conflicting, biased, incomplete information has bombarded us in recent years. We
have heard so much we don't know what we know! A quick
scan of newspaper headlines, magazine articles, and the titles
of popular books leaves one in a quandary as to whether we
should fear the Japanese or follow in their footsteps. Are
they bent on wrecking our economy to maintain their number-
one position? Or do they offer enlightened methods of production and management? Americans have been besieged with
an ever-growing barrage of Japanese success stories. More
often than not, these stories distort our understanding of the
Japanese business world, creating a glorified picture of Japan
as a land of King Midases where everything they touch turns
to gold.

A typical week's dosage of media events documents an out-
pouring of coverage on Japan-related subjects: an Irish psy-
chologist reports that Japanese children have a median IQ
score that exceeds that of their American counterparts by
eleven points; Sony Corporation has commissioned a famous
Japanese fashion designer to create a new company uniform
in celebration of its thirty-fifth anniversary; Corning Glass

Works has just bought a Japanese-based research laboratory from RCA; a new book reveals how De Beers, the famous South African diamond empire, and the J. Walter Thompson advertising agency created an overnight sensation by establishing the world's second largest market for diamond engagement rings in Japan; New York City's Metropolitan Transportation Authority purchases 325 subway cars from Kawasaki Heavy Industries in Japan, thanks to its American agent, Nissho Iwai; a New York cable television station is running an eleven-part series on Japan; and finally, we see newspaper reviews of the Tokyo String Quartet, and read that the famous Japanese movie *Eijanaika* and the well-known Japanese Noh play *Dojoji* are to be performed in Avery Fisher Hall, both on the same day.

From their sex lives to their business practices and management techniques, Americans are intent on discovering what kinds of "special powers" the Japanese possess—as if these "powers" promised some mystical energy or, if transported to the States, could serve as some sort of corporate aphrodisiac. Surely no foreign country has gained our attention so fast, been so revered, feared, scorned, praised, and misunderstood all at the same time as has Japan. It has become one of our more fantastic national obsessions, right up alongside dieting and video games.

The mass media have not been alone in their preoccupation with the Japanese presence. Serious academic debate has been raging over the feasibility of learning from the Japanese, of actually applying their production and managerial techniques to American firms. A cadre of scholars, serious journalists, and members of the business elite argue that if you can't beat 'em, join 'em. They are convinced not only that we should incorporate Japanese techniques into our business-labor model but that unless we do so, our industrial system, once the marvel of the Western industrial world, is doomed to languish in competition with the rising economic giant of the East.

Several serious books by well-respected experts in their fields have garnered the interest of many in the business and academic community: *The Japanese Are Coming, Japan as*

Number One, Theory Z, and *The Art of Japanese Management,* to name a few. Surprisingly, corporate America may even be taking a treatise on Japanese sword fighting—famous samurai Miyamoto Musashi's *Book of Five Rings: The Classic Guide to Strategy*—into boardrooms across the country. In addition to all this, a voluminous number of scholarly articles examining Japan's business success have been published in nearly every American consumer and trade newspaper and magazine. Hardly a month goes by without a "Special Report" or "Spotlight Japan" article underscoring the secrets" of their success.

The point has been raised by a number of astute Japan-watchers and business veterans concerning the viability of transplanting management styles and methods from the Orient to the United States. Can participative management Japanese-style work here? Can we import Japan's formula for high productivity into American factories? Is there really an "art" to Japanese management? Certainly there are cases where so-called "Japanese" techniques (usually blended with solid Western ones) have worked well. Sony's television plant in San Diego has long been enjoying laudable productivity rates. Westinghouse has for some time been experimenting with quality-control circles. A number of Japanese-American joint ventures are doing the same.

Too many questions concerning the viability of transplanting Japanese methods to the States, however, remain unanswered. Too many gray areas have yet to be considered and satisfactorily explained. Perhaps the best way to approach the "if Japan can, why can't we" issue is to recognize that there is no quick fix and clearly no single answer. Somehow an incorrect assumption has arisen that just because something works in Japan, it can work here, too.

Lastly, the influence of Japan has become a political issue further obscuring our perception of the Japanese threat. U.S. government officials and key political and business leaders, still smarting over a seemingly intractable trade deficit, are applying intense pressure on the Japanese to open their market to increased American and other Western exports. At home, politicians, responding to high unemployment due to massive layoffs in industries such as automobiles and steel, campaign by raising the "yellow peril" specter, winning support for government intervention to alter the lopsided trade pattern. Disharmonious economic competition has become a divisive political issue. Indeed, no nation can allow a gross trade deficit in Japan's favor to continue. No nation relishes Japan's economic potential to affect world business and set the agenda for the future of the industrial world. The Americans charge the Japanese with maintaining excessive and unfair tariff and nontariff barriers. Everyone's complaining about the invincibility of "Japan Inc."—the supposed economic matrix composed of Japan's major industries, government, and financial institutions—that is "devastating" foreign markets and industries.

The Japanese, on the other hand, are convinced of Americans' ineptitude or sheer lack of effort in successfully tapping into the lucrative Japanese market. They claim that America simply hasn't been trying hard enough and that the Japanese market is as accessible as most other industrialized nations' markets. Meanwhile, U.S. congressmen, pressured by their home-state constituencies, are crying wolf, claiming that the Japanese are destroying bedrock American industries. Unable to find a job in a depressed economy, Americans everywhere are demanding retribution.

The arguments are not totally in favor of either the Americans or the Japanese. For a long time, Japan has refused to address the political and economic problems that Westerners complain of, particularly the nontariff barriers and the problems of dealing with its Byzantine distribution system. On the other hand, there is truth to the Japanese claim that Americans haven't been trying hard enough, that they need to learn the ways of a foreign society if they hope to do business with it and to recognize that in order to meet the special opportunities and challenges in Japan, different strategies are required from those used in other countries.

The first step in learning how to do business with the Japanese is to look closely at those factors that cause even the best business executives to leave Japanese-American negotiations with a feeling of inadequacy and incompetence.

Objectives and Strategies: East Is Not West

A major difficulty in doing business with the Japanese is to adapt our business strategies to the Japanese context so we can achieve our desired objectives. The primary American *objectives* for doing business—to buy, sell, or negotiate a product, service, or idea—are remarkably similar to those of all business people the world over. The *strategies* to achieve those objectives, however, vary from culture to culture. Much of our international experience has been with Western Europe or former European colonies here in our hemisphere. Even though strategies differ from one Occidental nation to another, the overall difference is slight. The common cultural heritage we share with these nations allows us to adjust to the differences.

Now Japanese businessmen are testing our conventional assumptions regarding business principles and strategies. Even after the decade of the seventies, when U.S. trade with Asia surpassed our trade volume with Europe, we are still not certain which of our assumptions work, which don't, which need minor adjustments, which major revisions. Our experience with other nations in the West has conditioned us to expect quick, successful adaptations. But not so with Japan, whose cultural, social, political, organizational, even interpersonal dynamics are exceedingly different from our own. Most American business people still have grave doubts which of our business *principles* will work in the *reality* of the Japanese setting.

For instance, most of us learned the art of team negotiating either in college business courses or from practical hands-on experience. A shared set of premises about the etiquette and strategy of negotiating enables us to sit down at a table with complete strangers and initiate the proceedings that will hopefully achieve our own or our company's objectives. But the Japanese do not share these premises. They have different needs that operate in the process of team negotiations. For the American negotiator, there is a tremendous urge to seize control of the negotiations, be clear, make one's point frankly and precisely, and bring the meeting to a quick, decisive close. Sound familiar? It is in many parts of the world. Not so in Japanese companies, where the need to preserve group harmony is paramount. In order for all concerned to save face, Japanese negotiators submerge individual opinions and doubts in the group consensus. Instead of setting out with clear, decisive positions, a Japanese negotiator will create an atmosphere of ambiguity, even deliberate vagueness with its inherent deception, and avoid the strong personal initiative that characterizes the American style. In a group discussion, each Japanese is acutely aware of the Japanese proverb, "The nail that sticks up gets hammered down."

With such fundamental diversity in business strategies, arising from such fundamentally diverse backgrounds, will business with the Japanese ever be easy? The answer is probably not. When compared with the ease we have come to expect in dealing with other Western nations, the Japanese will always seem more difficult, requiring greater flexibility, more compromise, and greater ingenuity in adapting our conventional strategies to the realities of the Japanese business world. But there is reason to believe that Japanese-American relations will improve as more American business people learn the nature of the Japanese mind and become experts in the strategy changes needed for a meeting of the Eastern and Western minds in a business context.

Lack of Preparedness: No Time to Learn

Rethinking our business principles requires formal preparation prior to the initial meeting with the Japanese. Many first encounters get off on the wrong foot because of a mutual lack of readiness. Despite the obvious need, neither Western- nor Japanese-run corporations offer training programs on how to do business and how to better work with the other. In fact, the only real training that occurs is on the job, and that can take years and is often a rather haphazard approach.

In general, the Japanese seem better prepared than we are. They are more internationally oriented and hold a less myopic view of the world. They're more adaptable and eager to learn new ways and approaches, and assimilate these to their own. They seem to realize that we will be different; we seem to expect them to behave like us.

A thorough education in the Japanese character, their economy, their social mores, and their way of doing business is needed to produce an enlightened team of representatives from U.S. companies. There is much to learn, not the least of which is that the Japanese are no longer looking to us for models in the areas in which they already surpass us or feel confident that they will soon do so. We have reached the end of an era in which international business relationships were characterized by American superiority and leadership.

Some progress has been made. An increasing number of college courses are being offered to prepare lawyers, engineers, and business people in general in the theories and methods of Japanese business. By the mid-seventies, thirteen joint degree programs were established between professional schools and centers for Japanese studies. Thirty-seven universities offered courses in fourteen fields, including Japanese education, library science, and even agriculture. Yet this is just a small beginning.

The ease with which we have done business in other countries has been partially due to their willingness and need to learn from us. As Osamu Watanabe, director of the public relations division of the Ministry of International Trade and Industry, noted, "I . . . detect a supercilious conviction [among Americans] that economic prosperity and international harmony can only be brought about by Westernization of non-Western societies."[1] Clearly, the "supercilious conviction" must be eliminated.

The Communication Gap: Language and Logic

Another major barrier between the Japanese and American business communities is the communication gap. Communication is a two-edged sword whose one blade is language and the other logic. Years ago a missionary reported to his superiors in Rome that the "Japanese language must have been devised by the Devil to hinder the preaching of the Gospel to the heathen in Japan." Many modern business people in Japan must feel the same, only in this case the "work of Satan" is to foil American business ventures. Sadly, America and Japan have, among the world's developed countries, a low aptitude for learning foreign languages. Considering the fact that we do more trade with Japan than with any other overseas country, there is a disproportionately small number of Americans who are fluent or even semifluent in Japanese. If it weren't for the fortunate event that some Japanese— especially the ones that are sent on overseas assignments—are somewhat fluent in English, communication between the two nations' business communities would be close to nil.

While Americans lean toward learning Indo-European languages during their primary and secondary education, English is and has been mandatory in the Japanese education system. But Japanese is so phonetically simple, and American English so riddled with exceptions and alternate pronunciations, that the Japanese have great difficulty mastering it. Most Japanese rate their ability to master English rather low. The language problem can't be underestimated as one of the major obstacles in doing business.

The second edge of the communication sword is what Martyn Naylor refers to as the "logic gap": Japanese values and thought processes run parallel to those in the West, but never seem to meet or coincide with our own.[2] In order for us to be successful in dealing with the Japanese, we must realize that there are alternative logics to our own. Every culture is logical according to its own premises. Not every culture is based on the same premises about truth and reality as ours. But if we know the premises that our business partners and adversaries are operating on, then the way they think and behave becomes more comprehensible. For example, Japanese business people fail to see the importance of many things that are of paramount concern to Westerners: the nontariff barriers that keep American commodities out of Japan; the need for American companies to show quick, short-term profits; the desire on the part of many Americans to put their family and social lives first or at least on par with their work lives. All of these do not make sense when one understands the premises on which Japanese thinking is based.

We will explore in greater detail the nuances in Japanese logic and determine the key elements in the outlook of the typical Japanese businessman. This topic is the "hidden agenda" in each chapter of this book. Doing business with the Japanese is primarily a problem of understanding the Japanese mind, knowing the culture that produces that mind, and then learning successful techniques for appealing to the Japanese mind in order to reach your company's objectives.

In conclusion, one word of warning. Any treatment of national character—whether it be Japanese, American, German, or Serbo-Croatian—is bound to deal in generalities. The danger, of course, is stereotyping—which means to assume that a valid generalization about a group of people must apply to everyone in that group or that generalization about one characteristic negates others. Like Americans, the Japanese have their own personal idiosyncrasies which may have nothing to do with the fact that they're Japanese. Each person is unique and different. There are many exceptions to the images we derive of them, even images that are for the most part accurate. We must realize that while there exist general cultural behavioral patterns, people still should be judged on their own individual merit and not solely on the fact that they belong to a national group. Indeed, this would be a grievous error. And this is also the starting point of our discussion about the problem of doing business with the Japanese. Too often, the real problems are the illusions—the myths, the misperceptions, the stereotypes—that impair our vision of the Japanese and sabotage our efforts to relate to and understand our prospective business partners.

CHAPTER 2
Business by Illusion

IN THE HEYDAY of British imperialism, Rudyard Kipling observed, based on who knows what evidence, that "The Japanese should have no concern with business. The Jap has no business savvy." This comment has come to haunt our own business dealings with the Japanese. The spectacular results of Japanese business activity can be intimidating, and yet many Americans who attempt to transact business with the Japanese come away with a strong suspicion that, in spite of their impressive track record, Kipling was right. Is there a small oriental poem somewhere written by a Japanese poet that makes the same point about Americans? Do Japanese businessmen view Westerners with the same suspicion?

Cross-cultural observations are always risk-laden. And when other high stakes are involved, as in business, a wrong perception can be disastrous. Business based on illusion can lead to failure: the loss of time and money as well as deeply hurt feelings that might prevent both parties from ever considering future transactions. And yet misperceptions, superstitions, and stereotypes characterize an alarming number of transactions between Americans and Japanese—and threaten their chances of ultimate success.

Scene: A Conference Room

The Americans are anxious. Six months after an initial meeting, Osatech, the renowned Japanese video software company, has finally agreed to meet with an American negotiating team in its headquarters in Osaka. Videomart, number one in America's video-game industry, hopes to get a licensee agreement with the Japanese company to sell its software. The Americans should be anxious. Osatech has an impeccable reputation for creating one successful game after another. Landing a contract with it would be a real coup. Now, after what seemed to the Americans an eternity, Osatech has agreed that it is in the companies' mutual interest to meet and work out an acceptable deal—or so it seems.

The meeting gets off to a good start. After brief introductions and the ritual exchange of business cards, both parties sit down at the table, the Japanese on one side, the Americans on the other. On the Japanese team are the general manager, two assistants, and an engineer who will also serve as the translator. Representing the Americans are the president of Videomart, two vice-presidents (sales and marketing), and an engineer. They have no translator. Nor do any of the Americans speak or understand Japanese.

The Americans begin their opening presentation, giving a brief status report on their company, the amount of business it does, its share of the market, projected sales—a veritable "dog and pony show." They emphasize that Videomart has emerged as the industry leader in terms of unit and dollar volume. Repeatedly they point out that should the Japanese pass up the opportunity of doing business with them, the former would be doing their company a grievous disservice. After a lengthy public relations build-up, the Americans set the agenda, describe their product needs, suggest a time schedule and a delivery date. Item costs, they claim, can be resolved later.

During the Americans' presentation, the Japanese team has been quiet, listening attentively, occasionally nodding to one another. When the Americans finish talking, the Japanese ask many probing questions covering a wide range of issues—mostly in the category of detailed product specifications. They wish to see the engineering blueprints for these units. What about the new game Videomart plans to introduce at the next sales convention? May they please see a working model to check for compatibility? What about delivery dates? The Americans, taken aback by the nature of the questions, decide to call a recess to think through what has just occurred. The Japanese politely agree.

Alone in their conference room, the American team is aghast.

"I don't think they understood one word!"

"How do they expect us to tell them *that* when we don't even have a firm commitment from them that they will join us?"

"Nervy of them! They can't really keep asking questions like that without giving a few answers themselves. They just ignored you, Bob."

"Well, they kept nodding yes and smiling . . ."

"Yeah, but then they went right back to discussing things that had nothing to do with . . ."

"Or things we cleared up an hour ago."

"Look, no matter how it goes when we return, keep them off the delivery time issue until they've at least agreed in principle."

"Do you get the feeling that Yamamoto knows what we're thinking about? Why does he frown so often and whisper to his associate?"

"Does it everytime you ask him a point-blank question. Bizarre!"

"I get the feeling that he isn't really in charge of the final decision."

"Well, if he's not, who should we aim our pitch to?"

"Beats me. Maybe it doesn't matter. Talk to the translator, he's the one who . . ."

"That's what's bothering me. Everything the translator says is so vague and ambiguous. He's an engineer. He should know the technical terms."

"Maybe he doesn't know English very well."

'Well, they can't be noncommittal forever. They must know that other companies would give an arm and a leg to do business with us. They should know that, shouldn't they? Or . . . maybe they really don't know who we are."

· · ·

But the Japanese know very well who they are. In their own headquarters, they, too, are disturbed. Roughly translated from the Japanese, they are saying:

"I think it is all boasting."

"And rudeness."

"Yes, I'm not convinced we can trust this company."

"If they are as successful as they say, why must they criticize their competitors so frequently?"

"And why are they pressuring us? There are still many points to discuss—many points we still must consider."

"But they keep pushing on the same issues, asking the same questions over and over."

"They seem belligerent to me. I have never seen businessmen use such hostile gestures at a table before. And their obscure idioms are so difficult to translate."

"What part of the United States are they from?"

Two weeks and four meetings later, negotiations are even more mired in misunderstanding and suspicion. The Americans are flabbergasted.

"Can't they see what a lucrative deal this would be for them? And just think what the board will say if we don't come home with a deal!"

"We've been bending over backward, and where's it getting us? Just more meetings!"

"I'm getting sick of the stupid request to see our blueprints before we've even drawn up the terms of a contract. Remember that article in *Fortune* about Japanese spies in the Silicon Valley?"

"Yeah, well, what do you think?"

"I don't know. Two weeks and we've agreed to almost nothing."

"Would *never* have happened in Ohio."

The Japanese, too, are ready to pull out. To them the futility of doing business with these Americans is obvious.

"If they are sincere, why do they keep referring to their lawyers as if only lawyers can discuss and determine minor points?"

"They are not minor points, Yoshi."

"Yes, we know that, but they don't seem to."

"To me they are presumptuous and operate out of bad faith. They cannot be trusted."

"But their company can help us gain the distribution and market share like no one else, as they will not let us forget."

"I hope we do not have to hear that one more time. It makes me think we should consider doing business with another company that is not so 'tops.' "

There was one final meeting. It too failed. The Americans went home.

Shooting in the Dark

Two companies engaged in negotiating a deal that would have been mutually beneficial. Two companies operating in good faith. Two teams of professional businessmen. Why such a boondoggle? Why, when U.S. trade with Japan had jumped to over $60 billion, should two groups of businessmen flounder in their own inexperience to the point of failure? Why should both sides leave the table feeling that for several weeks they had been shooting in the dark?

The answer is that both the Japanese and the Americans in this typical scenario were doing business by illusion. Ironically, minds that should have met, since they were set on similar objectives, never managed to work through the strategies necessary for agreement. The sad fact, the ironic fact, is that no matter how highly trained and experienced these men were in their own businesses, within their own cultures, no one on either negotiating team had cleared his mind completely of the myths and misconceptions about his foreign counterparts.

After years of East-West trade, myths and misperceptions continue to be the driving force behind the derailing of many worthy business ventures. Going back to the days of the "yellow peril," the fears and suspicions lingering after Pearl Harbor and World War II, mutual distortions continue to blur American perceptions of the Japanese and theirs of us. Foreign trade arrangements are never easy, and they become virtually impossible when parties operate from ignorance, false information, and illusions.

Japan: A Favorite Nation?

Clearly, Japan is still not very well understood in the West. What Westerners do know seems to be either extremely negative or extremely positive. A handbook for business people on society and business in Japan points out that most Americans' attitudes toward Japanese culture and experience have often been superficial.[1] This includes our attitudes toward Japanese business success. Not only are our popular assumptions about it shallow, but they tend to be highly divergent. For example, some Americans think the Japanese achievements are due to their ability to imitate others, while others explain that the Japanese are innovative (but in their own way). Some Westerners emulate Japanese business techniques; others find them inscrutable and mysterious.

How do Americans learn about Japan? A 1982 poll by Potomac Associates asked this question of 1,006 adult Americans who picked from a list the one or two most important sources of information about Japan. Sixty-five percent learned from TV and radio; 53 percent from newspapers, magazines, books; 18 percent from purchase and use of Japanese products.[2] Clearly, the media comprise our chief source of knowledge about the Japanese. And how reliable are the media? According to a 1979 study, there are about 250 foreign correspondents working out of Tokyo, about five of whom can interview in Japanese! The rest must rely on interpreters who read Japanese newspapers to gather much of the information they relate to the Westerners, who in turn read the English-language newspapers printed in Japan. It is no wonder the study concluded that the reporting capacity of foreign correspondents is "quite limited."[3]

A certain amount of distortion occurs in all news reporting, whether by omission or by exaggeration. Akio Morita, president of Sony, told *Playboy* magazine in August 1982 of a typical use of omission by the American press. A U.S. congressman's racist remark about "little yellow people" made headlines in Tokyo, confirming what many Japanese believe, namely that Americans, even congressmen, are prejudiced. Morita pointed out that the incident was not even mentioned in the *New York Times*. He wryly observed that readers in Japan may know the names of senators and congressmen that the average American has not even heard of![4]

Regardless of what we know or how we learn about the Japanese, what do we really *think* about them? According to those sampled in the Potomac poll, Japan is well liked by Americans, ranking fourth after Canada, Australia, and West Germany. Sixty-three percent of the Americans polled held "very favorable" views of the Japanese; 29 percent held "somewhat" favorable views, totalling up to a large majority who think rather highly of the Japanese. And yet these figures represent a drop from 84 percent who had "very favorable" views in 1980 and a rise from only 12 percent in the "somewhat" favorable category. Clearly, while Japan still ranks high, there has been some erosion of esteem.

Recent trade policies may have hurt Japan's reputation. But that should be qualified: trade policies *as reported through the media* (where most Americans get their impression of the Japanese). In actual fact, Japanese and American trade policies toward one another have *improved* since 1980. But what the media choose to report becomes important in the popular mind, and focusing on the trade *problem* can cause many Americans to change their attitudes about Japan.

When asked whether or not Americans found the Japanese to be "trustworthy," only 15 percent of the Potomac respondents thought the Japanese were "very" trustworthy, while 50 percent thought they were "fairly" trustworthy, and 21 percent (or one out of five) believed them "not too" trustworthy. The pollsters interpreted this as a rather "cautious assessment" in regard to trusting the nation that ranks fourth on our list of favorite nations! Still, esteem for the Japanese runs high, and Americans are not making the Japanese a scapegoat for our own economic ills. Also, respect for Japanese products continues to soar unabated.

How do Americans describe the Japanese? According to a recent survey, on the negative side they are viewed as self-conscious, humorless, inscrutable, devious, shy, awkward in personal relations, vague, "economic animals," alien, imitators, and slavishly conformist. Favorable adjectives include talented, efficient, richly cultured, industrious, eager to learn, polite, and gracious.

From the Japanese perspective, Americans are unpredictable, arrogant, patronizing, ignorant of Japan, insensitive, and loud. More positive descriptions include likable, good sense of humor, pleasantly informal, competent, standard-setters, democratic, confident, modern, great achievers, and self-reliant.[5]

These descriptions are in part indicative of the numerous illusions and misperceptions that mar each perspective. Not every American nor every Japanese holds all these views. But this range suggests how easily positive or negative impressions of each other can easily arise. It is generally agreed, however, that the Japanese know more about us than we do about them. The Japanese are voracious readers of things American and worry unduly about what Americans think of them as a people. Shinsaku Sogo, a noted Japanese columnist, has pointed out that a quick glance into a Japanese bookstore would reveal a "huge number of books on 'American Impressions of the Japanese' that have been translated" into Japanese, some of which have become bestsellers.[6] Sogo ruefully admitted that after searching for thirty-four months in the U.S. to find a comparable book on what the Japanese think of Americans, he hadn't found even one. This knowledge gap is one of the major causes of false impressions between the two peoples and of course a major cause of the illusions upon which much Japanese-American business is conducted, and eventually founders.

Dissecting Illusions

The amazing fact about illusions and stereotypes is that thoughtful, honest observers on both sides can often see through them and yet remain blinded by them. How? Because at the core of every illusion is a kernel of truth. Sociologists who study the phenomenon of stereotyping explain that a stereotype (usually a negative characterization of a group of people) would not grow and thrive were it not for a modicum of truth. The old adage "Scratch a Russian and you'll find a peasant" (itself something of a stereotype!) might be adapted to "Scratch a stereotype and you'll find some truth."

Insincerity

In the scenario described at the start of the chapter we noticed that each side suspected the other of being insincere and dishonest—of operating out of bad faith. From the American point of view, what in Japanese behavior could be misinterpreted as insincerity? Most Americans would probably point to the "inscrutability" of Orientals that masks their true feelings. If the Japanese are being honest with us, why aren't they more open and frank? Why is their language so guarded, their statements so ambiguous, their faces so blank? Even the Japanese admit this accurately describes their behavior on many occasions, disclaiming, however, that this makes them inscrutable. Some Japanese, critical of the impression they create, accuse their own people of fostering an inscrutable demeanor that only befuddles and unnerves Westerners.

Take the smile, for instance. When it springs to the lips so frequently and without apparent cause, it does seem to suggest concealment. Shuzo Ishikawa points out that a Japanese will smile when he or she does not understand a question, rather than ask someone to repeat it, which they fear may offend. Sometimes the Japanese even smile when they are sad. Realizing that many foreigners take the ubiquitous smile to be mysterious and deceptive, Ishikawa believes that in some cases "the Japanese should abandon part of their culture or tradition . . . to make foreign people more comfortable."[7]

The same is true of the Japanese trait of saying yes. Since they hate to disagree publicly, they will frequently say yes even when they don't mean it. Ishikawa gives a clear and sobering example that should make every American business person pause to reflect. A Japanese asks another Japanese, "Aren't you hungry?" The answer is "Yes, I'm not hungry." To answer "No, I'm not hungry" (as we would do in the West) would express disagreement. Akio Morita also admits that Americans can get very confused over the Japanese use of yes and no. If a Japanese means no, he might say, "I will consider it." On the other hand, Morita claims, when a Japanese says to you, "I agree with you . . . then you still have much work left."[8]

Morita suspects that "we [Japanese] are not very experienced at expressing ourselves verbally." For the Japanese, sometimes silence is the best response. "We don't have to talk —just as between you and your wife or your lover."[9] As we noticed in our scenario, the Japanese sitting in silence so long infuriated the Americans, especially when the silence ended with a barrage of seemingly pointless or inappropriate questions. Jiro Tokuyama, the managing director of the Nomura Research Institute, told *Newsweek* that the Japanese have "traditionally looked down on verbal communication. . . . Even when there are conflicts of interests, the Japanese endure silence until they reach the breaking point."[10]

Many American business people think the Japanese take too long in verbal communications, ask too many irrelevant questions, or give quick, stock excuses when they themselves are put under the gun. They appear vague, indecisive, unsure of themselves—in a word, insincere. Takaharu Nikano of the New York State Department of Commerce told me that he thinks his countrymen are very "roundabout," that they don't clearly "define or express themselves." He says they'll never give you a job description, so it's hard to know what you're supposed to do. Kazuko Suzuki, owner of American-based

Suzuki Graphics, also thinks the Japanese "aren't verbal enough." They don't say what they mean or tell you what they want. On the other hand, Suzuki finds Americans to be excessively finicky over unnecessary details and notices that they, too, at times say yes when they don't really mean it.

In our scenario, the Japanese were upset that the Americans referred to so many "minor points" to be worked out later by lawyers. The Japanese have a distrust of lawyers that reflects what Dr. Masao Junikiro, anthropologist and adviser to former prime minister Takeo Miki, calls "a basic distrust and contempt for language as seen in the preference of many Japanese companies for unwritten contracts."[11] Akio Morita points out that the last paragraph of an agreement between two Japanese companies always says that if either company has trouble interpreting the agreement, "both parties agree to sit down again in good faith to discuss and renegotiate." Americans, of course, cannot understand this. If there is disagreement, there is little chance for good faith and so the last paragraph of American contracts defines a third party as arbitrator—or else we go to court. "In Japan we promise to sit down and talk. . . . That's the Japanese way," says Morita.[12]

In many negotiations the Japanese come across as two-faced or hypocritical, saying one thing, meaning another, doing something else. But veteran Japan-watcher Jack Seward notices that frequently the Japanese are considered two-faced *and* inscrutable—two characteristics that are somewhat contradictory! But then who ever said that illusions had to be consistent? Seward argues that being inscrutable goes back to feudal days when superiors demanded unquestioning obedience from inferiors. Most Japanese, being inferiors to at least one person, learned that a noncommittal inscrutability was better than showing their true emotions and risking severe punishment. Seward also explains that the Japanese have in fact many faces, not just two, and that to them this is not undesirable. In a highly status-conscious society, one should have different ways of treating the boss, the butcher, and one's brother. It is not hypocritical; it is just being differential.[13]

Former ambassador to Japan Edwin O. Reischauer commented recently that Westerners are often as inscrutable (and seemingly insincere) to Orientals as vice versa.[14] They often have a hard time figuring us out and what we're up to. Shuzo Ishikawa remembers a high school classmate saying to his friend after World War II, "I saw an American GI yesterday. I wonder what the Americans, behind those marblelike blue eyes, think, or, to begin with, if they can think at all."[15]

Rudeness

In the private discussions of the Japanese negotiating team, the Americans were criticized for their rudeness and excessive boastfulness. Courtesy—or the lack of it—is a stumbling block in Japanese-American relations. Japanese culture is layered with levels and degrees of etiquette that most of us cannot understand without firsthand experience. From the Japanese perspective, Americans are hard to "read" in terms of propriety because our democratic society has eliminated many formal indicators of status and consequently we have little practice in ritual formalities. The American way is to treat everybody pretty much alike; excessive formality is often seen as a sign of pretentiousness and insincerity. We do recognize propriety, but often find the clues subtle and hard to read when our expectations call for bold, informal behavior. For example, it is difficult for most American businessmen to discern where power lies in the Japanese corporate structure. The obvious signs of power are more subtle and hidden among Japanese managers, making it hard to really know who runs the show.

A frequent illusion created by the American style of conversation is that we lack all humility. We speak loudly and fast, and rarely say "I'm sorry"—a phrase that springs quickly and frequently to Japanese lips. Shinsaku Sogo's sardonic advice to Japanese is "when you arrive in the U.S. forget the words, 'I'm sorry' "[16] He recommends to his American friends that if they want to get along better in Japan, "use more freely the words 'I'm sorry.' " Even Americans whom I interviewed noted that very often in business negotiations, Americans overlook the human element. As a vice-president from Canon Corporation put it, Americans don't put enough emphasis on basic human respect, especially for one's competitors. This leads to boasting, which offends the Japanese. In addition, Americans value frankness and tend to be overly frank, saying what the Japanese consider to be the wrong things at the wrong time.

On the other hand, some Americans go to opposite extremes and try to outdo the Japanese in being polite. Overdoing courtesy—bowing and scraping, and in general trying to impersonate the stereotype of Japanese behavior—can make an American look like a fool. The Japanese respect Westerners more when they are themselves. Sometimes Americans speak simplistically to Japanese who they think understand little English. "You play golf?" "What your handicap?" Talking as one would to a child or an idiot creates the illusion of a condescending attitude toward the Japanese, who are adults and peers. The best rule is to talk slowly and avoid obscure terms and American idioms.

It's important to avoid bold, colorful language that might prove offensive. Morita remembers a man saying that "the Japanese are so stubborn that if you don't hit them with a hard punch they won't change direction, so let's give them a punch." "Sometimes people say such rude things," he added.[17] Unfortunately, even high-ranking public figures let slip comments which offend the Japanese sense of propriety. In the late seventies, former Treasury secretary John Connally was inclined to make the Japanese a scapegoat for many domestic economic woes. He got downright churlish at times, voicing what undoubtedly many Americans thought. "Don't they remember who won the war?" he was quoted as asking. During his short-lived campaign to be the Republican Presidential nominee in 1979, Connally regularly threatened Japan and remarked that if they weren't willing to abide by the "civilized" rules of international commerce (i.e., free trade), "they could damn well sit in their Toyotas in Yokohama and watch their Sony color TVs and leave us alone." This attack prompted Sony's president, Morita, to quietly contact Connally and request that he desist from his Sony comments since

80 percent of Sony's televisions for U.S. consumption are made in America.

Another sign of rudeness frequently not understood by Americans but commonly caught by Japanese is forgetting that age equals rank. Japanese companies are structured on a seniority system where, in general, age equals experience and promotion, so a handy rule of thumb is always to single out the older members of the group as the leaders and offer them the respect and deference due them, even though (as in our scenario) the leader himself will defer to assistants and those younger than himself for information.

In spite of their acute regard for courtesy, the Japanese themselves have several habits that Americans find discourteous. Chief among these is delineating degrees of friendliness based on status. To Americans, politeness should be dispensed equally, extended to all. But as Seward explains, etiquette in Japan is a "matter of demarcation. . . . Lines—many lines—have to be drawn."[18] This creates a situation of ins and outs that doesn't seem fair to more democratically minded Americans. In one respect, drawing lines is a safety valve in a society like Japan's where friendship creates extensive obligations and duties. The more friends, the more responsibilities, and so a rigid formula for courtesy protects everyone from the responsibility of having to treat all alike. Naturally, this conflicts with the American attitude that the more friends one has, the better, and contributes to a misperception by Americans that equates politeness with friendship. The two are not the same. What is perceived as friendliness should not be construed as friendship.

A related habit that appears to Americans as rudeness in many situations is that the Japanese speak Japanese to each other too much. "Too much" is a relative term, but at some point, Westerners consider the Japanese discussing business in Japanese in front of them as both rude and sneaky. It certainly doesn't square with our notion of frankness. Koso Takemoto, general manager of public affairs at Mitsui, admitted to me that he, too, considers it rude for Japanese to speak in Japanese while Americans are present. But again, it is a delicate matter of degree. A little consultation in Japanese is appropriate, but if it becomes excessive, it is rude.

In the aborted dealings described earlier, each side thought the other was not playing fairly nor acting in good faith. The Japanese thought it rude and unfair business practice for the Americans to denigrate their competitors and pressure the Japanese into making a decision before they had established a proper working relationship with the Americans. The Americans found the Japanese to be too nosy, secretive, deceptive, and slow to make decisions. In their minds, the Japanese were being rude in delaying and taking up time with unnecessary questions.

Superiority Complexes

Ironically, both the Japanese and Americans come across to each other as having an acute superiority complex. Many Americans have a "victor complex" that colors their relations with the enemy whom they defeated in World War II. Connally's "Don't they remember who won the war?" attitude is typical of many. For years even before the war in the Pacific, Americans viewed themselves as the center of the world, assuming that other nations should look to the U.S. for political, economic, and social leadership. However, the Japanese rise to dominance in so many areas of industry, technology, and trade has produced in them an arrogance that often creates ill will. In part their expressions of superiority may be due to their need to overcome their sense of inferiority from having lost the war. But even before their military defeat, the Japanese had their own "better than thou" self-concept. Professor Donald Keene of Columbia University, lecturing at a Japanese-U.S. forum in Osaka, pointed out that the Japanese are often glad to find something a foreigner doesn't understand so that they can show him or her how it's done. Traditionally, they have prided themselves on having a unique appreciation of certain foods, arts, and social graces, such as painting, gardens, flower arrangements, tea, etc. Recent discussions in America about applying Japanese management techniques and learning from them have intensified this feeling of superiority.

So we have the volatile situation of two highly advanced cultures with built-in superiority complexes, each misjudging the other, each expecting the other to humbly submit to the other's needs and demands. Who has it worse? It's hard to say, but as Keene pointed out, Americans are never surprised to see Japanese businessmen wearing Western suits, whereas an American in a kimono always looks a bit peculiar to the Japanese! That might tell us something. Indeed, it is difficult for the Americans to reveal humility, to show weakness, to admit ignorance. A senior vice-president at Dentsu Advertising admitted that problems arise when Americans and Japanese workers are engaged on the same project because the American usually takes the "I'm right, you're wrong" attitude which offends Japanese co-workers. On the other hand, Denise Hamilton, an American employed at the Japanese trading company Nichimen, found the reverse of this in her own experience. She thinks that many Japanese have the attitude that precisely because we are Americans, we will never understand!

It's important for Americans to realize that the Japanese have a superiority complex and that, like ours, it is a handicap to personal relationships that is hard to overcome. Leonard Silk of the *New York Times* claims the Japanese desire to be best can be seen in their "highly nationalistic and mercantilistic approach to trade" where they perceive trade "as a form of combat in which they are determined to win"[19] Of course, they take great pride in winning and expect others to treat them as winners, especially in areas where they are number one or close to it.

Americans often find the Japanese very unbending, wanting to do business their way or no way at all. Jiro Tokuyama gives us an insight that might help us understand this rigidity. He explains that typical Japanese have a very insular mentality reinforced by school, family, the agency or firm—not to mention the island itself—that prevents them from seeing others' points of view. After years of living and working in an enclosed, elite atmosphere, the average Japanese has "never experienced what it is to be on the outside. Few of them understand the feeling and thinking of people outside their own close-knit groups."[20] And what's worse, they attribute this attitude to outsiders as well. In other words, as Donna Levis, formerly employed at the Japanese publishing company Dempa Shinbun, notes, many Japanese think that *because* they are Japanese (i.e., different, insular), no one will ever understand them. Since they think it's impossible for others to ever know what it's like being Japanese, they often see no point in trying to explain. Nevertheless, they still give the impression that they would like others to do things the Japanese way!

The Japanese as Imitators

It is certainly no illusion that the Japanese are great imitators. They have taken Western technology, adapted it to their own needs, improved upon it, and even exported it back to the West, making considerable profits in the process. Clearly, it is not unprofitable to be able to imitate artfully and successfully. But the perception that they are *only* imitators is an illusion. Equally illusory is our incomplete understanding that fails to attribute other valuable qualities to the Japanese, like creativity and innovativeness. For example, a 1982 article in the *Economist* shows that the Japanese excel at teamwork, the ability to learn from others, and persistence in incremental improvements—all values that the West appreciates.[21] And even though these traits are unexciting, they are the very requirements that contribute to innovation.

Author William H. Forbis suggests that "one by one" the Japanese are "ordinary people" and often convey the impression that they lack flair or brilliance. But "as a totality . . . the Japanese excel."[22] So when Americans work with individual Japanese workers, they get the impression that the Japanese are mediocre, lacking in original ideas, and slow to grasp analytical concepts. Henry Kissinger once noted that it was difficult to demonstrate things to the Japanese because, in his words, "They have no notion of causality . . . no conceptual thought. They can't make an outline."[23] Naturally the Japanese resent attitudes such as these. As the *Economist* article further explains, economic success has given the Japanese a terrific sense of pride and self-confidence. To be considered nothing but copycats is a charge that rankles them. It would be similar to ignoring the Romans' tremendous achievements in engineering, law, and world government because they borrowed many ideas from classical Greece. Perhaps as Americans we should keep in mind that Henry Ford did not invent the automobile. The French did.

It's true the Japanese don't completely understand American logic. Even the Japanese admit an inability to follow analytical, linear reasoning. As Yoshimichi Yamashita, president of Arthur D. Little in Japan, put it, "The Japanese fundamentally cannot absorb the methodology of analytical, scientific thinking per se."[24] Why not? Several explanations have been offered by the Japanese themselves. One is that the Japanese educational system emphasizes rote memorization rather than analytical thinking. Children are trained to memorize truth rather than to discover it by independent thinking and problem-solving. The Japanese language may also have a lot to do with it. Dr. Makoto Kibushi, Sony's research director, suggests that Western children learn to put one letter after another, then one word after another word, and in the process learn how to think linearly, a style of thinking necessary for logical deductions. In contrast, the Japanese ideograms do not require the eye to follow the pen sequentially. Hence the Japanese child learns to recognize *patterns* of meaning, not *lines* of meaning.

Robert Ballon, a Jesuit professor who has lived thirty-five years in Japan, explains another trait that gives Westerners the impression that the Japanese lack creativity. The Japanese tend to look just one step ahead and are satisfied with small improvements, whereas the Westerner frequently tries to predict the future and develop new, outlandish concepts even when there is no practical use for them at the moment. Ballon claims that the Japanese consider it a waste of time and energy to look too far ahead.[25] Much better to focus on small changes that will have some impact today.

The Japanese themselves realize they are not great innovators and often present an image to the rest of the world as being inherently slow, unanalytical, and not given to inventive genius. But they have initiated changes to correct that image. Japanese firms now give "VP" status to research directors, a clear signal that research (inventiveness) is a way to reach the top. Japanese universities are opening their doors to Western professors in the hope that they will help Japanese students to learn how to think independently. Similarly, Japanese scientists, who are isolated from the international community, are being sent abroad to study and teach at foreign universities. The Japanese believe that, given time, changes such as these will erase the illusion shared by many outsiders that the Japanese can't "think" like Westerners.

Work Perceptions

It is reasonable to expect illusions to arise as the Japanese and Americans view each other as co-workers. Even in a homogeneous group of co-workers or colleagues, there is misunderstanding and lack of acceptance of each other's habits, methods, and styles. In a cross-cultural setting, however, there is even more room for misperception since work habits and values are largely conditioned by the culture one grows up in. It is difficult for people transplanted into a foreign work environment to adapt easily or to understand their alien colleagues.

In general, our perception of the Japanese is that they are "workaholics." Sometimes it is put more favorably: they are a "disciplined work force" or exhibit a "loyal devotion to the employer" or a "traditional work ethic." The Japanese seem to have not yet discovered the clock and the standard quitting time of five o'clock. Frank Gibney describes the Japanese work environment as a "kind of transistor-operated anthill."[26]

Whether they work harder or not remains to be seen. Certainly Japanese workers look busier, an impression fostered by the fact that they tend to work in groups. Professor Ballon believes the Japanese consider "living" to mean doing some kind of work and points out that, not having our Judaeo-Christian background, they do not think of work as divine punishment for original sin.

However one explains it, the Japanese attitude to work and their work style are different from ours. How, then, do they perceive us?

Basically they find us somewhat lazy. They think we watch the clock in order to leave at quitting time to go home and be with the family where life really takes place. Sogo points out that most of American life is centered on the individual and the individual's family, especially the mate.[27] Many Japanese can't understand why we prefer home life over business.

Another characteristic that bothers the Japanese and creates a negative image of us is our mobile work system. It is not uncommon for an American to change jobs several times in the course of his or her life, whereas many Japanese employed in larger firms usually stay there until they retire. Our system creates the illusion that we are an unstable, volatile work force that cannot be relied upon. One high-ranking Japanese in Dentsu Advertising thinks that hiring Americans will hurt the company because of this restlessness. It also fosters the attitude among Japanese who hire Americans in whatever capacity that we are akin to temporary clerks who come and go without making strong commitments to the company. If this notion spills over into action, it is easy to see how ill feelings can erupt between Americans and Japanese even when their responsibilities are on the same level. Mike Tsukamoto, director of the Japan Electronics Bureau in the U.S., thinks that because American companies fire employees who are not performing well, the Japanese have the impression that ther are fewer guarantees and less stability in American companies than in Japanese firms. It's therefore hard for American companies to get good Japanese employees since most would prefer to work for Japanese firms with their built-in guarantees. Consequently, many Americans hire Japanese to work for them simply because of their ability to speak English rather than because they have the proper skills for the job.

American individualism seems opposed to the idea of teamwork. A corollary to the lack of team spirit is selfishness. Many Japanese interpret our desire to do jobs alone or be alone as selfishness, particularly in light of their extreme sense of teamwork. It's been pointed out that Americans have a penchant for private offices and love to call people in to have meetings. How contrary to the Japanese who work in groups and across from each other. Even the department manager or group coordinator works in full view and shoulder to shoulder with his subordinates. At any rate, it is important for Americans to dispel the illusion of laziness and selfishness on the work scene in whatever ways they can.

Economic Relations

As we saw earlier, there has been a slight erosion in American perceptions of Japan since 1980, attributed by pollsters to the media's emphasis on poor economic relations between the two countries. Some of this slippage in esteem is due to our trade imbalance and high unemployment in the U.S. Forty-four percent of Americans think Japanese imports contribute "a great deal" to American unemployment, and 37 percent think it contributes "some." It would seem that Americans are quick to attribute our economic ills to Japan. And yet the same poll shows that we are not setting Japan up as a scapegoat. In other words, there are other culprits as well as Japanese imports. A series of questions covering this problem indicated that Americans were looking inward as well as outward for causes of the trade problems. When asked to rank the following factors in terms of importance, the results were:[28]

	VERY TRUE	SOME-WHAT TRUE	TOTAL
1. Japanese wages are lower than American wages.	64%	22%	86%
2. American workers are not as productive as Japanese workers.	39%	27%	66%
3. The American economy is in bad shape with low rates of investment and equipment that is out of date so we can't compete.	36%	30%	66%
4. American businessmen don't try hard enough to enter the Japanese market.	22%	33%	55%
5. The Japanese market is closed, and Japan restricts imports.	23%	29%	52%

Though there is a feeling that conditions in Japan are a major cause of our troublesome economic relations, Americans are not absolving themselves. A majority of Americans polled, 57 percent, said the U.S. and Japan are "equally" to blame; 31 percent thought the U.S. mostly at fault.

Yoshi Tsurumi, professor of international business at Baruch College, thinks it is quite understandable that Westerners fear an invasion of Japanese and Japanese products. For the first time in history, a non-Western nation has "become affluent and somewhat arrogant in mass and has gone multinational in direct competition" with American and European nations. He thinks that resentment of Japanese proliferation around the world is likely to rise, not subside, in the years to come. Japan has "many idiosyncrasies that baffle and irritate foreigners." He thinks it normal that foreigners have "paranoid fears of Japanese coming in droves."[29]

Mike Tsukamoto believes that Japanese companies are definitely "more secretive than American companies" on trade reciprocity and that even though the Japanese say that their markets are open, in actual fact there are considerable barriers. He thinks "very few Japanese know what they're talking about" when it comes to rectifying existing trade barriers with the U.S. Still, Tsukamoto doesn't believe that the Japanese government could force the doors open. There are just too many other variables over which the government has little or no control.

Images of the "ugly Japanese" have replaced the old image of the "ugly Americans" riding roughshod over the economies of other nations as they stake out their territorial claims around the world. Shuzo Ishikawa urges his countrymen to eliminate prejudice wherever they can by educating others *and themselves* concerning the problems they are creating.[30] Seeing trade as a type of combat, the Japanese have unquestionably alienated many people who should be treated as allies rather than adversaries. Leonard Silk reports that even some Japanese businessmen "now feel Japan may have focused too narrowly on its self-interest and they think the time has come for Japan to behave as a better world citizen."[31]

Conclusion

On the whole, the picture many of us have of the Japanese is based partially on reality and partially on myth and misperception. Together myth and reality create illusions that hamper smooth-working business relationships. When people conduct business by illusion, one or both parties are bound to feel cheated, manipulated, deceived. It's no wonder so many Americans and Japanese do not understand one another. The person they are trying to understand is partly illusory. We are as inscrutable to them as they are to us. Throwing up one's hands and crying "they're inscrutable" is no substitute for the strenuous, self-critical effort needed to penetrate beyond illusion and stereotypes to a genuine understanding of each other.

CHAPTER 3

The Japanese Company at a Glance

A THIRTY-TWO-YEAR-OLD Ohioan with an MBA from Columbia University went through the initial "getting to know you" period when she went to work for Mitsubishi International Corporation (MIC) in New York. It seemed to her that she would be getting to know them forever. Kazu Hikida, MIC personnel manager, explained, "Her boss expected an MBA to be brilliant, have close Wall Street ties, and come up with a creative money-raising idea a week." And true to the form of most Japanese managers, he expected her to understand her duties just by being there and taking part in the group. So he explained very little to her. Another recruit who joined MIC in Atlanta was told explicitly what to do by his manager: forget everything you learned in school. "We'll teach you the way we do it here, he said. There were no books or manuals. He taught me from his own history."[1]

"Book-learning," as they say, is never as good as on the spot experience. True. But being prepped about the nature of Japanese companies and how they operate can make doing business with the Japanese (and going to work for them) a less frustrating experience. This chapter, like a street map for an unfamiliar city you intend to visit, will show you the highlights, the major avenues, and points of interest that you should be familiar with when dealing with a Japanese company. While it's true that no two Japanese enterprises are exactly alike, especially when comparing a company in Japan with a subsidiary in the U.S., there are common elements. Japanese companies employ similar practices, have analogous structures, and share a good number of spoken and unspoken rules and taboos. This chapter will give you a brief overview of:

- the much-discussed "corporate and management philosophy" that supposedly accounts for smooth internal operations,

- the key characteristics of management-employee relations that some advocates are recommending for American companies,

- techniques the Japanese company uses to network with other firms and business partnerships to do business both in Japan and abroad, and

- the unique problems and challenges facing Japanese companies in America.

Whether we like it or not, the Japanese are here to stay. Every month new Japanese concerns open up somewhere in the U.S. The results of a 1978 study by the Japan Society, aptly titled "The Economic Impact of the Japanese Community in the United States," gives a good indication of the profound repercussions the presence of Japanese business has had on our economy:

Japanese investments in 1,177 business entities in the U.S., employing approximately 10,500 Japanese businessmen, exceed $3.4 billion.

Japanese firms manufacture an estimated $4.8 billion worth of goods in the U.S.

Japanese companies in the U.S. create 261,000 jobs for Americans, including 127,800 related to the goods and services the Japanese must purchase from Americans: 63,900 jobs in law, accounting, and advertising, and 64,100 in the public sector.

Japanese firms pay $885 million in taxes each year.

Japanese firms import approximately $12 billion worth of consumer goods for sale in the U.S.

The $6 billion worth of Japanese-manufactured automobiles imported into the U.S. created an estimated 113,500 jobs for Americans in sales and dealerships.

Japan is the largest source of overseas tourists to America. There are almost one million Japanese visitors to this country each year, spending an estimated $540 million and utilize the services of at least 24,800 Americans employed in the restaurant, hotel, and recreation industries.

One-Room Beginnings, Imperial Endings

The widespread influence of Japanese companies in America may come as a surprise to many, but some of these enterprises have been around a long time.

When Sony's current president, Akio Morita, made his first trip to the U.S. in 1953 representing a company then called Tokyo Tsushin Kogyo, he quickly discovered that "no American could pronounce our name correctly."[2] He and his colleague sat down with several different foreign language dictionaries and came up with the root *sonus*, which means "sound" in Latin, checked it out with other major languages, and renamed their company Sony. Ten years later they showed their first profit. The rest is history.

Panasonic started in radios in the late 1950s out of a two-man sales office. It has since burgeoned into a giant U.S. sales subsidiary that today sells more than six hundred products in the U.S. and is a significant portion of the parent company in Japan that sold more than $15.6 billion worth of products in 1981 alone.

Toyota is another example. When the firm first arrived on American shores, its chief executives knew little about making cars for American consumers, let alone selling them in a foreign environment. America's Big Three car manufacturers never even considered the newcomer a serious threat. But the Japanese were willing to wait—and learn. The current president of Toyota and another top manager went to work for a Ford factory for eight months to learn the American methods of organizing an assembly line and the kinds of problems they could expect to meet and solve in competing with American cars. Like Sony, Toyota took about ten years before it really began showing results. And clearly it has shown results!

Today these modest one-room companies have grown into worldwide empires, and Morita and other pioneer businessmen like him are rightfully proud of the way they entered, survived, and in many ways came to dominate their markets. It was long, grueling work, requiring years of patience. No wonder Morita counsels American businesses that success in foreign cultures comes only after a long struggle and much patience. There were no quick fixes when it came to studying specifications to meet popular American tastes, learning what safety features were required by government regulations, determining the most effective advertising themes.

What are the dynamics, the stamina, the tactics that account for the solid success achieved by Japanese companies and their subsidiaries in America? Let's take a closer look at the internal workings of a typical Japanese company.

Corporate Culture: Ideas You Can Work By

On April Fool's day an American company in California served its employees raw fish and provided them with specially crowded commuting facilities. Yes, it was a joke. But in very serious ways American firms are beginning to "go Japanese" as they realize the value of having and exploiting a "corporate culture." For years McDonald's has promoted "QSCV"; quality, service, convenience, and value. IBM has had the slogan "IBM Means Service" (they also have a company song, "Forever Onward, IBM"). And Delta Airlines has promoted the "family feeling." And there is always the "Go to it, girls!" attitude of Mary Kay Cosmetics. But behind all the glitter and lyrics, what exactly is a corporate culture?

It's something Japanese companies have had for a long time, naturally, spontaneously, and profitably. A Mitsubishi

Man is not a Matsushita Man! And the Japanese workers—
reportedly—know the difference. Is it merely that workers
behave the way they think the company expects them to behave? Not just that. As Robert H. Waterman, author, management consultant, and promoter of the corporate-culture
concept for American firms, points out, it includes beliefs,
values, and loyalty as well as action. While songs, rituals, and
morning calisthenics are important, the Japanese have discovered that by training a work force that really *believes* in
what it is doing (i.e., what the company is doing) production
is better, quality improves, and employees are generally happier at their work. Waterman suggests that each company
should promote its distinct identity and tone so that Americans
can begin to create that same commitment that Japanese workers have toward their companies.[3]

The Matsushita Creed

The creed by which a company operates and expects its employees to function can sometimes be spelled out in great
detail. Consider the following code enunciated by Matsushita
Electric Industrial Company. It may sound strange to Americans who cannot fathom what philosophy and poetic idealism
have to do with automobiles, steel, and electronics.

Progress and development can be realized only through
the combined efforts and cooperation of each member
of our company. Each of us therefore should keep this
ideal constantly in mind as we devote ourselves to the
continuous improvement of our company.
1. Objectivity: Power or profit cannot be our only
goal in life. First we must unselfishly contribute to the
betterment of our community and nation, then profit and
growth can be our expected reward.
2. Fairness: No person can ever earn the respect of
himself or another without practicing the principle of
fairness. Wisdom alone can never replace human under-

standing. But both can produce satisfaction and happiness.

3. Togetherness: Individuality will never overcome the strength of totality. Dependence is a virtue, trust is a necessity. Only then can true harmony exist, flourish, and prosper.

4. Accomplishment: Self-reliance always breeds self-respect. Complacency is never a sound substitute for constructivity. But progress results from desire and dedication to succeed.

5. Humility: Every individual should always remember his own humble beginning. Egotism will never outpace modesty and true encouragement is the bridge between failure and success.

6. Adjustment: Change is inevitable. Resistance is the reflection of shortsightedness. Without freedom or flexibility, we will always stumble rigidly forward and unhappily out of step.

7. Appreciation: The greatest human reward is simply a kind word. Consideration creates closeness. Recognition causes respect because tyranny will never replace thoughtfulness.[4]

The Human Connection

Basically, the sense of corporate culture rests on the human connection that, on the whole, Japanese companies express better and more genuinely than American companies. Tanemichi Sohma, vice president of administration at Sanyo Manufacturing Corporation of America, criticizes Americans for missing the human part of "human relations." Very often the attitude of management and worker is that the only link between them is a cash nexus: hardly a human connection at all. The boss pays the worker for a job; each gets just what is expected, and nothing more. Not so in a Japanese company. Richard Johnson discovered that Japanese companies spend "significantly more on non-task, non-payroll related company benefits"[5] compared with American companies. A great deal of the money goes into social and recreational opportunities for employees. Sanyo, for instance, gave new workers transistor radios and a 7 percent bonus its first year in the U.S. to boost morale. It is common for companies to have recreation facilities on the grounds and weekend retreats for employers and employees located off the premises for picnics and family gatherings. Sony, like most other companies in Japan, supplies its people with work clothes, including three jackets. In the U.S., Sony and many other Japanese subsidiaries sponsor baseball, football, bowling, and other activities on a regular basis. They consider this an important dimension of corporate life, a chance for employees of various backgrounds and departments to mix and socialize in a structured and acceptable way. Nomura Securities provides its five thousand female employees with skirts, blouses, vests, and jumpers, in both winter and sumer fabrics, and pays the cleaning bills to boot!

The virtue which pervades most Japanese relationships, whether business, social, or familial, is *amae*—indulgence, protection, concern for one another. All their lives the Japanese are conditioned to show *amae* and receive it. This carries over into working relationships as well and can be seen operating between managers and their staffs and between co-workers on every level. Specifically, it expresses itself in an indulgence that tolerates others' idiosyncrasies and foibles, respects the other as a human being, and makes sincere efforts to protect others from mistakes, losing face, or bearing the blame for errors. In some ways, it is similar to the American "united we stand"—a sentiment not applied very often between labor and management and not always among workers themselves either.

However it is expressed, the sincere concern for the individual is paramount with the Japanese, and great efforts are made to unite management and employee with bonds of devotion, idealism, commitment, and just plain good fun. When it's time for the company softball or volleyball game, it is normal to see top-level executives and assembly line workers on the same team. In general, the distinction between management and worker is not as extreme in Japanese companies as it is in America.

Management: The Human Contact

It comes as a disturbing surprise to many Japanese employers to discover that in America "older" is not always "wiser." When experienced American managers in their forties and fifties were hired by Japanese companies, a good number of them failed by Japanese standards of management. Their résumés looked good; they had the necessary qualifications; they had excellent recommendations. But they didn't always work out. What did they lack? They weren't harmonizers. They couldn't get along with people very well. They turned out to lack interpersonal skills. The Japanese were surprised because one just doesn't survive in Japanese society without interpersonal skills. But in America, business management has not placed priority importance on this, and as a result a large number of American managers, even with considerable experience, simply can't cut the ice in a Japanese company. It has been suggested to Japanese employers in the U.S. that they should test an applicant's "interpersonal suitability" before hiring him.[6]

In Japan the manager is foremost a harmonizer, or as Peter Drucker puts it, "a human contact, a listener, a guide for young people during their first ten years or so in business."[7] The manager is a father figure, someone who can differentiate his people's individual talents and needs and motivate them to do their best. He's like the conductor of an orchestra. He maintains morale. As Akio Morita explains, if the manager "wears a white overcoat and never goes to the factory," if he "sits in a beautiful office, while the factory workers work in a poor environment," morale is bound to be low. Production will fall off; quality will be jeopardized.[8]

Beyond the Buck

Maintaining harmony between the upper echelons of a company and the lower-level work force is important, and the
Japanese have discovered that rewarding excellence and good
service with salary increases can unwittingly disrupt that
harmony. Resentment over salary differences can breed ill
will. Rewards other than money are offered in a Japanese company, rewards such as authority, respect, enhanced reputation.
Tanemichi Sohma correctly identifies the theory underlying
this practice as a form of Skinnerism. Reward correct behavior and thinking with peer recognition and eventually one
desires to do well in order to be well thought of. Respect and
recognition—they aren't bought with dollars as in America.
They're *earned*. In fact, a president of a Japanese company
makes seven to ten times less money than his counterpart in
America. His reward is the reputation he has achieved for
himself over many years of devoted service to the company
and to his fellow workers and colleagues.

Whether or not instilling a corporate culture in American
companies is feasible remains to be seen. Most consultants
agree that action and lip service without belief is meaningless.
American workers will have to take the company philosophy
to heart, and to eradicate the widespread cynicism that under-
lies many Americans' attitudes toward company philosophy.
American companies will have to come up with a philosophy
worth taking to heart. If nothing but company profits moti-
vates the owners and shareholders, there is not much hope
that American workers will respond positively to ideals such
as those enunciated by Matsushita.

The *Ka*

Unique to Japanese companies is the *ka* or work group. People never work alone in Japan. A typical work group is composed of about fifteen members of various ranks and levels

plus the *kacho* or chief. Invariably, the work group will become one of the most important groups in one's life, next to one's family and friends. When one is placed in a work group, it is not because of particular skills, but because of one's ability to be trained. In fact, while in the work group, a person is expected to learn and perform more than one task. The work group takes full responsibility for the jobs assigned to it, so no one person is at fault if the project fails. Likewise, praise for work well done goes to the *ka* and not to individual people.

A person is transferred from group to group over the years and thus has a chance to work with several *kachos*. Each *kacho* evaluates his workers and makes recommendations regarding what positions and tasks an individual is suited for. The *kacho* himself has had at least fifteen years of experience before being selected as chief, so most are in their late thirties and early forties. Promotion in general for Japanese employees is automatic by seniority. It is not linked to job responsibility or any special achievements. One might be inclined to expect a lot of sloughing off among workers who do not have to work for rank and higher salaries. And indeed, human nature can take the easy way out even in the pressure-cooker atmosphere of a Japanese company. Knowing they will not be fired unless they are a true disaster to the firm, some lifetime employees get the reputation of being "sunshine boys." They sit by the window, figuratively speaking, and soak up the warm sunshine while younger employees, still proving themselves, buzz around the office doing most of the work.

But in general, the Japanese are hard workers and high achievers. There is intense peer pressure to do a good job and demonstrate to the *kacho* and your fellow workers that you're a vital employee. Word gets around and, as we've seen, peer recognition plays a crucial role in motivating the Japanese.

A tremendous sense of teamwork arises from such close working conditions and shared responsibilities. Everyone knows what job objective the work group has and is familiar with most of the individual tasks related to the objective. In addition, all the members know the status of the group's progress, know who's doing what, what's been accomplished, and what remains to be done. Meetings are always open, everyone hears what's being discussed. The Japanese desire for consensus keeps the decision-making alive as points of disagreement are ironed out. Everyone feels free to offer suggestions and all opinions get a fair hearing. Consensus is a perfect way to force people to agree and get along. There is a lot to determine within the group because the boss delegates a great number of duties on a kind of ad hoc basis as needs arise. The situation is fluid and ever-changing, unlike the American system where prior decisions frequently determine who will do what and when. The intensity of interaction and discussion is mind-boggling to Americans.

One of the traditional features of the decision-making process in a Japanese company (less so in American subsidiaries of Japanese companies) is *ringi*—a process where all members of the work group formally make and document their decisions. A proposal written out on a *ringisho* will be circulated among all individuals involved in the decision, including higher-ups. As each person reads and approves the proposal, he affixes his seal to the document (sometimes sideways or upside down if he doesn't actually approve). By the time the *ringisho* has made the rounds it has the appearance of a group decision with all parties concurring. The *ringi* process, however, can take some time, much to the dismay of certain businessmen who expect decisions to be made quickly. There is nothing you can do to speed up the process short of sneaking into the workers' offices at night and stamping each one's seal on it!

Job Rotation

Mitsuji Muraoka, a fifty-year-old division manager for Mazda (Toyo Kogyo) has worked for the company for twenty-six years. In his long career he has been an accountant, a plant designer, an efficiency watchdog, a materials-handling specialist, and a computer systems manager. Did he have trouble finding his niche? No. His career is not unusual. Most Japanese workers are rotated from job to job every three to five years to learn various aspects of the company they work for. There is disagreement in America on whether this produces mediocre generalists or versatile, interchangeable workers who can step into almost any job where they are needed. There are definitely advantages to job rotation, however.

It prevents the creation of narrow specialists who know only their field. It allows Japanese workers to meet a wide variety of fellow employees in other departments and divisions of the company. It also produces a work force that is intimately knowledgeable about the company, how it works, what kinds of activities contribute to the final product or service. A Japanese worker has greater appreciation for the totality of the firm he or she works for and comes to understand what other people do and the problems that they face every day. Furthermore, job rotation prevents the inopportune loss of skilled workers since there are always others in the company who can step in in times of illness, death, or unexpected absence.

Probably one of the most attractive benefits of job rotation is that the Japanese worker makes contact with other people in the company. These friendships can be useful later, either at work or recreation, or in one's social life. The Japanese worker thus knows actual acquaintances who give life to the concept of company philosophy. It is not just a vague idea or creed that he knows only as it applies to his own desk or work bench. He can see and feel the collective effect of it in his associates. It is embodied in real people, some of whom are his friends.

Quality Circles

In the work group, in job rotation, Japanese workers continuously come into close contact with other employees and learn the unique problems and challenges of other facets in the corporate community. One thing they learn early and for which they are expected to assume responsibility is: quality. Not left solely to managers, quality control is a joint responsibility. A unique form of participatory management has been devised to ensure worker input in solving problems that arise in quality control: the quality-control circle.

Quality circles are groups of usually ten to fifteen people involved in similar areas of work who meet regularly to spot problems and pool suggestions on how to solve them. The advantage of quality circles is that many problems can be nipped in the bud, while more serious ones can be analyzed from several points of view. Often the solution will be a combination of approaches that could only be derived from several minds working on it simultaneously. The use of quality circles also says to the employee that he or she has something to contribute to solving operational problems. The employee is not treated like a pawn, good only for carrying out the decisions of management. A company that utilizes circles experiences a definite change in the quality of working life, as American companies that have tried them have discovered. Morale is boosted, employees have a greater sense of self-worth, and individual participation increases understanding and commitment to the company.

Quality circles began in the 1960s when the Japanese decided to change the negative image of Japanese products as poorly made, toylike items that would not last very long. The concept of quality circles was a national strategy to convince consumers around the world that Japan could produce high-quality and durable merchandise. It is estimated that today in Japan there are about eight million workers participating in over 600,000 quality-control circles. In America in 1982 there were approximately 6,380 circles, but the movement has apparently stalled as Americans discover it is not the panacea they had expected. In fact, some complaints suggest that they are time-consuming, expensive to initiate (usually with fees to consultant firms who set them up), disruptive of normal work routines, and relatively useless in solving major problems. Part of the problem is that American management, while giving lip service to the idea of circles, does not always relish sharing the decision-making process. Furthermore, there is a growing resentment among some Americans at being told that they should do things the way the Japanese do. Japanese managers of American subsidiaries point out another factor that can make or break the quality circle in an American setting: the lengthy re-education of American managers. The decentralization of the problem-solving process requires extensive sharing of privileged information in order to devise solutions. Many managers are reluctant to share such information or, in fact, have little authority to do so.

The Old Suggestion Box

Suggestion boxes have been around a long time. You can tell how long sometimes by the amount of dust on the lid. But to illustrate how Japanese workers take an interest in the decision-making process in their companies, consider the suggestion box at Matsushita. In one year the 6,500 workers stuffed their suggestion box with 85,000 suggestions! That's almost 233 suggestions a day, or more than one suggestion a month for each employee! However you look at it, the success is phenomenal. In fact, it was such a success that special filtering committees had to be formed to process the suggestions, select the better ones, group those that were related, get back to the people who originally made them, and ultimately put into practice the ones they thought would work.

Panasonic, an American subsidiary of Matsushita, tried a suggestion box with less than spectacular results. Even with large cash incentives of 10 percent of the value of savings resulting from the suggestions, up to $10,000, the company's thousands of workers came up with only *forty* suggestions in a year. Is it that Americans don't have any ideas about how something could be done better? Hardly. Or is it that Americans don't generally think their suggestions will be taken seriously by management? Most likely. It's interesting that the cash incentives offered the Japanese workers at Matsushita were not nearly as large. But what happened was that workers pooled their ideas and the money they received, then held parties for themselves or, in the case of those with substantial winnings, took a weekend at the company resort.

Lifetime Training and Lifetime Employment

When Peter Drucker, the American management aficionado, was visiting a Japanese firm and tried to make an appointment to see the president, he was informed that a particular time of day was out of the question because the president had his regular welding lesson then.[9] You're never too old to learn in Japan, the nation of samurai warriors who spent their entire lives practicing and perfecting swordsmanship, calligraphy, and judo. With such variety and challenge, there is probably not very much of what has been recently identified in the West as "job burnout."

Men and women employed in the large firms are generally assured lifetime employment until age fifty-five, at which time they are usually rehired in some lesser capacity or part-time position. Most Japanese workers claim they like the security, accept the fact that they will work for the same company for most of their lives, and are willing to be retrained and reassigned within the company as the need arises. In fact, there must be a willingness on the part of employees to perform various tasks and a willingness on the part of management to retrain workers for the job security concept to work.

A Japanese electronics company in California is explicit about the need for its workers to be ready and willing to fill any post that needs filling or to do any job, no matter how menial. Its in-house newsletter put it this way:

"When there is a need, we all rally to meet it and consider no task too menial or demeaning: all that matters is that it should be done! We are all ready to sweep floors, sort parts, take inventory, clean machines, inspect parts, load trucks, carry boxes, wash windows, file papers, run furnaces, and do just about anything that has to be done!"[10]

In addition to having this jack-of-all-tasks attitude, Japanese employees must also be ready to accept wage cuts during hard economic times or even a four-day work week.

All this may sound cumbersome to Americans, but many Japanese believe that the lure of permanent employment attracts better workers. Since promotion and raises are based on seniority, there is not the restlessness found among Westerners to move on to something better. Japanese workers, as a rule, don't feel caught in a dead-end job since job rotation keeps things fresh. And even if you're stuck as president of the company, there's always welding! In spite of the fact that his future is claimed by one company, the Japanese worker remains optimistic that the advantages outweigh the disadvantages.

The Darker Side

It has been pointed out, however, that even with its low rate of unemployment, between 2 and 3 percent in 1982, Japan is not really a worker's paradise. Agricultural workers, of course, do not enjoy the benefits of those who work for the large prosperous companies. Smaller firms cannot promise lifetime employment and, in fact, hire a good number of temporary workers. There is quite a bit of job changeover in the middle- and small-size companies where conditions are not as secure, and there are not the plush fringe benefits found in the large conglomerates. And as Japan's economy continues to stagnate while its burgeoning growth rate is beginning to peak and level off, companies are already becoming burdened with a large work force that can't be laid off very easily.

Japan Inc.: Myth or Monster?

It has become popular to refer to our Japanese competitors by the term "Japan Inc."—a concept that conjures up a leviathan-like corporate monster, poised with money, strategies, marketing objectives, a bureaucracy staffed with sharp-shooting financial wizards, and a boardroom inhabited by representatives of Japan's major banking institutions, powerful industrial groups, trading companies, and business associations. The chairman—to extend the analogy of Japan, Inc.—would be the Japanese government's Ministry of International Trade and Industry (MITI). Compared to American business, the phenomenon of Japan Inc. looks truly alien and formidable. To a remarkable degree, the Japanese have been able to achieve a unity of purpose unknown in America, where business, labor, banking interests, and foreign policy aims are often at loggerheads with one another. Instead of discerning the many Japanese companies, groupings, and individuals that do function on their own, Americans have tended to see only a "single actor, Japan, whose behavior resembles that of a corporation," as Bruce Cummings describes it in a special report for the *Nation*.[11]

But is this the reality? Not entirely. There still remains fierce competition within Japan. Stockbrokers, companies, banks, and even MITI do not operate with the singleness of purpose that we would expect from many of the reports about them. MITI has not worked out as well as planned, according to Tom Lifson of Harvard University. Not all companies are the same even though they share a similar structure and behavior pattern. Ken Ohmae advises us that if we want "to understand why Japanese companies do so well on world markets, it's important to recognize that they have built up their competitive strengths in perhaps the world's most competitive domestic marketplace."[12] In other words, it is the "need for survival" that accounts for much of the Japanese company's success, a concept that should not be alien to American ears still tuned to our own sagas of the wild frontier and the winning of the West by American ingenuity, technology, and industry. We can share with them the Darwinian world view.

The *Sogo Shosha*

An area where the Japan Inc. phenomenon appears to be truly formidable is the *sogo shosha,* the powerful Japanese trading companies, some of which trace their international connections back over one hundred years. These global networks of people, offices, and information banks, with their thousands of contacts both formal and informal, provide the many services that can facilitate trade for their clients, the private Japanese businesses and industries that rely on advice and direction from the *sogo shosha* for their international business ventures. As one official corporate brochure spells it out, the "purpose is to facilitate and develop trade flows and industrial activities at both the international and domestic level." Styling themselves differently from companies that are user- and maker-oriented, they see themselves as "supply-demand oriented and function as problem solvers."[13] Originating in 1868, these trading companies evolved from handling 1 percent of the exports in the Japanese cotton textile industry to commanding 80 percent of all Japanese cotton trade by 1918—quite a leap in fifty years. With the spectacular growth of Japanese industries and trade in recent years, these trading companies now not only handle import-export matters but are "extending their roles as trade and finance intermediaries in domestic industries and foreign countries."[14]

Today they are a major force in expediting Japan's world trade. They gather information and statistics, spot trends, and make predictions about new markets and products that they share with client companies. They know where certain products can be sold, how to get them there, what distribution systems must be used, what prices will most likely be, and on and on. And their services extend far beyond Japanese clients. The Mitsubishi International Corporation, for example, expedites Saudi Arabian oil for Japanese buyers, imports shoes from Brazil for Sears and Thom McAn, and exports soybeans from the American Midwest to Western Europe. In short, these trading companies are like the central nervous system of much of the world's trade. And in some cases, the brains as well. As we engage in ferocious competition with companies who enjoy the services of the *sogo shosha*, we have come to see that, if we are to compete successfully, something like an American *sogo shosha* is needed.

In the fall of 1982 the U.S. government passed a law to loosen antitrust prohibitions and allow American firms to create trading companies modeled on the Japanese *sogo shosha*. Sears and General Electric among others are now doing so, basking in the new law's leniency on forming closer associations between banking institutions and various industries for the purpose of beefing up foreign trade. Prior to this law, such activities would have been illegal, clear violations of the antitrust laws.

Does this mean that the old antitrust bias of the West is becoming obsolete? Hardly. Antitrust legislation continues to deter coordinated activities perceived to be a threat to the competitive ethic of capitalism. Recently twenty-seven Japanese paper manufacturers and trading companies on the West Coast were accused of illegal price-fixing. Deciding what prices they would pay to American woodchip sellers, dividing the market among themselves, allocating U.S. sellers according to their individual needs—all of this smacked of unfair play, and the woodchip dealers brought suit. Clearly, the American belief in free trade, rugged individualism, and competition finds such business coordination suspect.

Negotiated Interdependence

If Japan Inc. is more myth than reality, what then actually exists on the Japanese business horizon which we in America perceive as the mirage of Japan Inc.? Are we merely hallucinating? Or is something really there?

Perhaps a more realistic way of understanding Japan Inc. is in terms of "negotiated interdependence." Even with the fierce competition inside the Japanese domestic market, there is a strong need to respect and work with each other, a sense of teamwork that extends to the large network of banking, financial, industrial, trade, and business groups. This need to work with other companies and to subcontract phases of production has created a basic trust and understanding among the individuals involved. Another example of interdependence: it is common for Japanese firms to get long-term bank loans, which allows them to drop their prices when they are faced by a decline in demand or by overproduction. Nor is it uncommon for a company to have credit terms ranging from 100 to 180 days. The need for this kind of coordinated behavior has resulted in the negotiated interdependence that makes the Japanese nation such a formidable economic adversary.

The mutual understanding between industrial entities even allows them to conduct much of their business without the need for lawyers and written agreements. This has engendered and reinforced an atmosphere of consistency and reliability between firms. Many reputations have been built up over the past hundred years, beginning during the days of the original uncensored Japanese trading companies. It is a well-acknowledged dictum among Japanese businessmen that this trust must not be violated. The only negotiated interdependence that will work is based on trust, understanding, patience, and good will—terms that seem to be so much fluff to hard-nosed Americans. But it is not fluff to the Japanese. It is the iron network of understanding on which the concept of Japan Inc. rests. And it works.

Organizational Development Departments: The Missing Link

An important arm of the typical international Japanese company is the Organizational Development or OD department that functions as an advisory office, monitoring transactions between the subsidiary companies and the parent company. As Yoshi Tsurumi explains them, they have no "direct profit responsibility." Their primary function is to maintain records and evaluate the performance of overseas subsidiaries. They handle the individual needs of companies and employees, their tasks including matters as diverse as arranging travel services and shipping "care packages" to Japanese nationals stationed overseas and hungering for Japanese items they can't get in the foreign country.[15] One of its more important and often overlooked functions is helping overseas employees maintain their corporate connections, which may later prove crucial if the employee is to reenter the parent company in an advantageous position.

Using techniques gleaned from the behavioral sciences, OD personnel plan change within a company in light of that company's individual culture and the need for the corporate culture to adapt to the national culture of the country that hosts its subsidiaries. In other words, these enlightened facilitators act as the "missing link" between parent company and subsidiary, paving the way for long-distance adjustments needed for successful ventures. OD departments are also responsible for drawing up operational budgets and planning many of the international activities of the firm. Obviously, a division not worried about profit and having access to the budgets and activities of other divisions both at home and abroad can swiftly facilitate planning, make perceptive decisions, and advise other departments on matters in their best interests.

The Japanese company has developed a unique ability to survive temporary setbacks and losses for long-term gains in the international market. In fact, market acceptance is more crucial to the Japanese than profits in the initial days. Akio Mikuni, a financial consultant, was quoted in the *New York Times* as saying that "Profit in Japanese is not really a good word."[16] You will find the Japanese company willing to cut prices and accept short-term losses in order to corner a larger share of the market. One of the reasons for this is the different and less influential role that shareholders play in the Japanese company. Takayuji Nakajima, a senior economist at Daiwa Securities, claims the "Japanese stockholder is nothing."[17] Since most of the operating funds a Japanese firm relies on are from banks, not stockholders, the company can operate without alienating shareholders and without being embarrassed about not turning a substantial profit on their investments.

The Japanese Company in America

In America the Japanese company is faced with many challenges: Americanization, unionization, bad media coverage, the need to compete in an economy that is undergoing serious and unpredictable changes, an occasionally unfriendly government, and sometimes actually hostile legislation. But the Japanese are resilient, as history has proved; they are great borrowers and adapters. They do their homework well, collect as much information as possible, and usually rise to meet the challenge. As Hirotaka Takeuchi from the Harvard University Graduate School of Business Administration said at a 1982 conference on Japanese companies, their attitude is "do it, fix it, try it." There are no magic recipes for their success or for meeting the challenges that lie before them. If we can judge by their past record, they will stress key business values—service, quality, employee interaction, cooperative management—and they will please their customers. There is a certain purity about this simple formula and the lean stance that the Japanese assume. They stick to what they know best. If they make steel, they make steel. They don't buy publishing houses.

The Japanese Businessman in America: Trials and Tribulations

The Japanese businessman in America experiences the usual culture shock one would expect when hopping hemispheres. In addition, he is caught *between* cultures, still owing allegiance to the parent company and yet under pressure to meet the demands of the subsidiary which must come to terms with the American society in which it hopes to operate. Like any stranger in a strange land, the Japanese feels disoriented, unsure of himself, and tempted by a lifestyle that he knows is at odds with his traditional upbringing and value system.

For example, the *amae* that we have seen as endemic to Japanese society has few counterparts in America. Without this sense of being nurtured and indulged, Japanese businessmen can feel extremely lonely in America. They find American relationships cold, distant, temporary, conditionally determined by the needs of the moment. In Japan relationships are characterized as "*hada* to *hada*" (skin to skin), what we would mean by "heart to heart" perhaps, expressing a willingness to be sincere and open with one another. Unfortunately, the largest Japanese community in America (40,000) is stationed in New York City, a city not noted for "*hada* to *hada*"!

The Japanese male is also disillusioned to discover that most American women do not find him sexually appealing, preferring, as they do, taller men with Occidental features. Compounding this problem is the typical Japanese man's lack of experience in socializing with women. For many married men their last period of heavy socializing with women other than relatives was before the wedding. After that, the women in their lives tend to be wives and geishas in the hostess bars, both playing subservient roles that do not prepare the Japanese businessman for the independent, outgoing women he will meet in America.

Language is a major isolator. Not being comfortable with American idioms, no matter how much they have studied formal English in school, most Japanese tend to be cliquish and spend time in social clubs or piano bars and Japanese restaurants where they can use their own language. These places become welcome refuges from the carelessness and rudeness they see expressed daily by waiters, taxi drivers, sales clerks, fellow workers, and other Americans who treat them brusquely and exert little effort to help them with language difficulties.

Another alienating factor in America is the litigious quality of so many relationships and situations. America has about one lawyer for every 450 people, compared to Japan where there is one lawyer for every 10,000 Japanese. A statistic such as this clearly reflects the American concern for legal rights, which sharply define many relationships in the U.S., both professional and personal. The Japanese, on the other hand, are less concerned about legal rights and duties and what's legally mine or yours than about the quality of a relationship in terms of longevity and mutual supportiveness. Knowing how litigious we are, the Japanese in America are wary of entering relationships that can be dissolved as easily as two parties pull out of a contract or take each other to court.

On the positive side, the Japanese businessman here feels a sense of liberation and freedom from the strict code of conduct he is expected to live and work by in Japan. He discovers that American companies encourage initiative, personal creativity, and individual thinking. He can be himself here and engage in self-expression on a scale not possible in the Japanese work group back home. Should he become accustomed to this freedom, there is also a strong temptation to join an American firm and stay here for good. Doing so, however, is tantamount to being ostracized by the Japanese community. In fact, the more "American" a Japanese becomes while here, the more suspect he is among his peers.

So he is caught, trapped in a new environment that can destroy his old values and expectations and that liberates new feelings of individuality and self-expression. Even the Japanese who did not want to come here in the first place (and many of them never wanted to) but were sent because of special talents or the need for training, find their loyalty tested at some point in their American tour. Some do remain and become American citizens. Others, thoroughly committed to Japan, bide their time and eventually return to their homeland. In either event, the trials and tribulations of being in America create psychic strain; and under constant pressure, they lead rather stressful lives.

Growing Resentment

Resentment of the Japanese influence in America is growing and takes various shapes and guises. An antitrust suit has been brought against Japanese-owned paper companies on the West Coast. The federal government has warned the New York City Transit Authority about purchasing subway cars made in Japan when American companies are struggling to stay alive. A Reagan administration policy raised tariffs on Japanese motorcycles tenfold in order to bring relief to the last American cycle manufacturer, Harley-Davidson Motor Company. A sex discrimination case against a large trading company, Sumitomo Shoji America, resulted in the Supreme Court deciding that a Japanese subsidiary in the U.S. is an American company and must follow hiring practices as regulated by the Civil Rights Act. Three Japanese auto makers (Honda, Toyota, Nissan) enjoyed combined profits from imports in 1981 of $890 million at a time when the American automobile industry, in the doldrums, reported an aggregate loss of $1.34 billion. An FBI sting produced accusations against the Mitsubishi company of having illegally obtained information from IBM, a scam that former prime minister Zenko Suzuki, addressing the Japanese parliament, called "really a shocking event." And William F. Baxter, President Reagan's assistant attorney general for antitrust matters, when asked if joint research and development projects, such as Japanese firms have begun, would violate antitrust laws, replied that "it is important to maintain rivalry in the process of innovation" and that if companies got together for R and D projects, they would "be deprived of any individual incentive to steal the march on . . . competitors."[18]

Counterattack

Rumors, gossip, innuendos, as well as hard, bitter court cases: however their reputations are tarnished, it hurts the Japanese. Paramount to them is the necessity of saving face and being well thought of. To cope with the generally bad press the Japanese presence in America has been receiving, a new publication, the *Journal of Japanese Trade and Industry*, has hit the newsstands. A slick, glossy, sophisticated magazine reporting on developments in the Japanese business communities around the world, it is in fact an instrument of propaganda from the government's Ministry of International Trade and Industry. Osamu Watanabe, director of the ministry's public affairs division, admitted the slant the magazine uses in presenting a more favorable picture of Japanese business ventures. "It is a magazine of MITI. And its shadow chief editor is me."[19] Aiming to ease the mounting trade friction, the forces behind it hope it will contribute to a more balanced analysis of the problems Japan has with her major economic partners. The magazine itself is a classic example of the Japanese willingness to look for long-term effects rather than short-term profits. When asked if the magazine will show a profit, Watanabe replied, "No, only losses"—although he secretly hopes that someday it will be profitable. Someday.

Neither Fish nor Fowl

The Japanese company in America has more than an image problem. It has an identity problem as well. Is it Japanese or American? How fast and to what extent should Americanization take place? Specifically, at what pace should American managers be given more responsibilities? How should Americans' demands for equal treatment in job rotation and career training be met?

The options that the Japanese management faces are difficult ones. The company either becomes American from the start, or it becomes a company with a great many American employees grumbling over a code of ethics and work that they can't understand or believe it. If Americanization occurs at too slow a pace, Americans sense that they are working for a transplanted alien firm that is slow in taking root on U.S. soil. Compounding the problem of setting guidelines for Japanese companies is the fact that different industries have different needs. It has been estimated, however, that a rate of 80 percent Americanization in the first three to four years is one which satisfies both Japanese management and the American staff.

There are risks in Americanization. Mitsubishi Corporation discovered that its Americanization strategy cost them some of ther Japanese clients who either set up their own trading companies or, worse, went into partnership with a rival trader that had not Americanized to the extent that Mitsubishi had. The challenge for companies engaged in Americanization is to hold onto old customers at the same time as they generate new business and adapt to the peculiar needs of the host country. There are no easy answers.

American Managers: What Price Equality?

"For the first time many of the Japanese are confronted with the evidence that some of their colleagues are not as smart as the Americans." Professor Yoshi Tsurumi believes that the week-long seminars he runs for Japanese and American businessmen are slowly eroding the general disdain that many Japanese have for their American counterparts.[20] There are various reasons for this disdain, cultural as well as professional. But perhaps, as some observers are suggesting, a good deal of it is also personal. Japanese stationed in America see the growing Americanization of their companies as a threat to their own role. What will happen when the prestige management positions currently filled by career-minded Japanese are filled by Americans? Many fear the loss of job opportunities for themselves. Some genuinely fear the loss of the Japanese style that they believe is so important for success. How will their companies fare when Japanese employees are replaced by seemingly loud-talking, brusque, self-oriented American managers who have never learned the art of interpersonal relations?

Where and when to place Americans in management positions is a delicate question for Japanese companies in America. It is fairly well assumed that the top position of president should go to a Japanese from the parent company. The work force, of course, is predominantly American. But who should be second in command and what about middle management positions? A recent study showed that in regard to the choice of second in command, the best results were seen in firms that had a Japanese national from the parent company as vice-president. When this position is filled by an American without the security of lifetime employment, he tends to please the Japanese plant manager and in the process "screen[s] out important complaints from the American staff below."[21]

Another problem confronting Japanese management in America is to what extent the company should follow the system of job rotation as it is practiced in Japan. A JETRO (Japan External Trade Organization) report advised downplaying job rotation after interviewing companies that tried it. Comments such as the following came from management that found American resistance to the system. "Americans generally prefer to become excellent in a single kind of work. They don't like to do various types of work—it makes it difficult for them to change jobs." Many found the job rotation theory in direct conflict with another basic principle of Japanese management: personalized respect for the needs of the individual. "We respect the wishes of the individual. We do not force rotation on him," replied one manager.

The Problem of American Labor Unions

There is a world of difference between Japanese and American unions. In America workers want their unions to take an adversarial stance against employers. The history of labor in the U.S. is filled with riots, violence, bloodshed, and a long, hard struggle over a hundred years to win the respect and rights they have today achieved. In the process American unions found that the best results came from workers organized in trade unions that spanned individual companies. In fact, the company union idea has been sneered at by many as tantamount to no union at all. The situation is far different in Japan. Unions are usually organized by company, and since in many cases the workers have a guaranteed lifetime employment with the company, the union and company are compatible bedfellows. When strikes occur they last about one day. In America a strike can drag on for weeks or months, sometimes necessitating the involvement of the local and federal authorities. For Americans, the specific demands are important, and the American worker is usually willing to stay out on strike until the demands are met, or partially met. In Japan a "let's-have-a-strike-and-get-it-over-with" attitude produces strikes that occur mainly out of principle, to make a point about labor conditions, but strikes seldom last long enough to hurt or cripple the company.

There have even been remarkable (from the American perspective) cases of a union cooperating with management in ways unheard of in our country. Mazda, for example, was headed for bankruptcy when the high cost of fuel oil dampened customer enthusiasm for the rotary engine they were producing. Rather than allow the company to go under, the union encouraged its members to do anything necessary for survival. The result was that some auto workers left the assembly line and went out as salesmen to push their cars that weren't moving off the lots. Again, an ingrained willingness to be retrained and to perform a variety of tasks for a company rather than just one's specialty contributes much to the color and tone of Japanese labor unions. As Tanemichi

Sohma of Sanyo views it, the issue of human relations makes the difference. A feeling of oneness with others in the company, a concern for the employees' welfare beyond the paycheck, and a working relationship with many employees throughout the company allow union members to consider and work for human issues rather than merely economic ones.

The Japan Lobby: A Little Help from Their Friends

Yes, the Japanese are here, and it seems they are here to stay. Whether one believes in the control and influence of Japan Inc. or not, Japanese companies linked to one another by mutually negotiated interdependence, helped by powerful worldwide trading companies, and headed by strong-minded, patient "survivors" like the pioneering Akio Morita, are a fact of American economic life. Agencies like JETRO (Japan External Trade Organization), EIAJ (Electronics Industry Association of Japan), MIPRO (Manufactured Imports Promotion Organization), and others helped pave the way for new companies to enter the American market. Fact-finding studies to inform Japanese companies about the problems of locating here are being produced each year by these researchers who survey and report in minute detail the conditions that new Japanese companies will have to face and surmount. Even various state Departments of Commerce have set up offices in Japan in order to better attract Japanese companies and manufacturing operations to their respective states.

A new and powerful Japanese lobby in Washington has also been assembled to facilitate more and more Japanese companies' entrances to the U.S. Comprised of only seventeen agents in 1977, the Japan lobby now includes over 140 people with high-placed and influential friends both in government and key businesses. People like Frank Church, Robert Strauss, William Colby, and Brock Adams, to name a few, are actively involved in the delicate negotiations between the two nations, their governments' decisions that will prove either favorable or unfavorable to one side or the other, and the pressure that American and Japanese businesses can bring on all concerned to effect an outcome both sides can live with. Colby is quoted as saying that foreigners "on a safari in the American political system . . . need a local guide."[22] Their local guides have helped the Japanese cut through the undergrowth of the often confusing power structures in the U.S. Their safari is succeeding beyond the wildest expectations of the Eastern—or the Western—imagination.

CHAPTER 4

An Insider's Guide to Excruciatingly Correct Behavior

KNOWING HOW TO behave with the Japanese goes far beyond the proper way to handle porcelain chopsticks, the best way to dip your sashimi, or whether sake is sipped or swallowed. No, the issue of business etiquette comes down to knowing the fundamental and pragmatic aspects of transacting business. At stake is how best to elicit a positive response from the Japanese and how to avoid no response at all; equally important to the Japanese are the proprieties and formalities that accompany business transactions. They may not be matters of substance to you, but they are to the Japanese.

Bending with the Wind

Cracking the Japanese code of conduct often seems more difficult than cracking the espionage code Japan used to send military secrets during World War II. In doing business with the Japanese, it is important to demonstrate that you understand, respect, and can accommodate yourself to their code of conduct—without sacrificing your own personal and professional integrity.

Every business transaction requires a certain degree of adjustment, compromise, flexibility—concessions we don't always want to make but that may become necessary if the transaction is going to succeed. Some Americans with a touch of Archie Bunker's xenophobia are easily intimidated by what appears to be the "inscrutable and bizarre" way the Japanese do business. They either ignore it or feel superior to it, either way giving the Japanese the impression that we have a condescending attitude toward them. Consequently they never win the trust and confidence the Japanese expect and rely upon in business partners. Other Americans attempt to out-Japanese the Japanese, beat them at their own game, by bowing and scraping to excess. Quite frankly, neither approach works.

The Japanese recognize and accept the fact that we are Westerners—after all, that's one of the reasons they want to do business with us. And just as you expect them to be Japanese, they expect you to be authentically, but not obnoxiously, American and to act according to your own code of conduct. At first you may have a natural inclination to ape the Japanese manners and mannerisms. It's somewhat normal to spontaneously assume the characteristics of someone you are trying to make a good impression on. But overdoing your Japanese act or trying to conform completely to what you think is the Japanese way of doing things will surely make them suspicious. They'll probably find your behavior bewildering and insincere.

While maintaining your own professional integrity, you must overcome the myopic mentality that sees only the American way of behaving and learn what the Japanese consider correct and acceptable behavior. It does not mean that you have to do everything the Japanese way. It simply means that you must understand and utilize their etiquette strategically for achieving your own goals and objectives. If you have had relatively little exposure to foreign cultures, adapting to the Japanese may be difficult at first. But the more experience you have with them, the more insights you will derive into why what appears as inscrutable behavior is really a justifiable, socially useful, and necessary way of life for the Japanese.

Shrewd Perceptions

The astute negotiator will be aware of subtle, nonverbal cues in facial expressions and hand gestures that may seem innocuous, but are actually meaningful signs. A slight intake of breath before a Japanese says "yes" may mean "no." When the Japanese moves his open hand, palm facing left, in front of his face with a back and forth action as if he were fanning a fire, he indicates a negative response to another Japanese. This occurs frequently when one Japanese wants to indicate to another that the foreigner with whom they are speaking probably doesn't understand the language well enough to catch on to what is being said. Another nonverbal indicator is laughter, which Jack Seward explains can mean "embarrassment, confusion, shock, and even grief" to the Japanese, whereas Americans usually interpret laughter as mirth, derision, relief, or scorn.[1] Americans, too, have nonverbal ways of saying things, but they are not always the same as the Japanese. Sometimes we shake our head, roll our eyes upward, and "tsk" to indicate disbelief in someone else's comment or behavior. Our American colleagues quickly read the message, but people from another culture may miss it altogether. Similarly, we must become more adept in reading the subtle behavior cues of the Japanese, or we run the risk of constantly misinterpreting what is being conveyed.

Seeing through Stereotypes

When observing a group of foreigners, we frequently spot the stereotyped behavior we are looking for. But there is more going on than what we see, and on closer inspection we will realize that not all the members of a group, even though displaying outward similarities, are alike. The same is true of the Japanese. One Japanese salesman for a large high-technology company and a veteran of dealing with Westerners, expressed his irritation with Americans who stereotype him as a Japanese fresh off the boat. "I've worked and lived here for fifteen years and have an American wife whom I met at Columbia University. At this point in my life, I'm closer to my American friends and associates here than I am to my friends and family back home. Yet I still get the old clichés thrown at me about 'How do you guys do it?' and 'What's your secret?' when I get into conversations with Americans about the Japanese economic miracle. People always ask what it's like being Japanese and how I'm adjusting to the customs here or how well I speak English. I still have to accept compliments about how my accent isn't so bad! Really, you'd think I'd just stepped off the boat!"

What's important for Americans to realize is that some Japanese are more Westernized than others and should not be treated like their counterparts who have spent their lives in Japan. The Japanese individuals one encounters often break that stereotype in one way or another and turn out to be just as variable as Americans. After all, even the "slow-talking Southerner," "the abrasive New Yorker," and the "plastic New Age Californian" are also stereotypes appearing more frequently in the imaginations of journalists and sociologists than as one's neighbors or business associates.

Looking-glass Behavior

Like Alice in Wonderland, sometimes travelers in foreign countries need to do the exact opposite of what is considered proper behavior at home. The situations where Westerners are most conscious of this reversal in dealing with the Japanese are those involving the written word and logic.

Western businessmen have a strong need for clarity, for preciseness, for getting details and directions letter-perfect. In many situations the Japanese prefer and often demand ambiguity and vagueness. Westerners need to adjust to this preference and realize that it would be futile attempting to pressure them into being more precise, or definite.

Decision-making is a clear example of this. When Americans make decisions in groups, it is important for everyone to understand the details, objectives, and goals, and to work out compromises and strategies, the overriding imperative being that all of this should be clear. When the Japanese make decisions, they tolerate much ambiguity and vagueness, and many loose ends. For them, ambiguity preserves an arena for discussion and disagreement, for airing opinions, for getting issues out on the table so that eventually a consensus may be reached. Ambiguity plays a crucial role in preserving group harmony for the participants in the decision-making process. So just when you think no one is taking a definite stand or agreeing to anything of substance, and you're ready to throw in the towel, remember that from the Japanese perspective, the meeting is not a failure. To them, progress is slowly being made through the chaos of ambiguity.

Another typical Western prejudice concerns logic and rationality, qualities often considered indispensable to successfully negotiating a business deal. This approach almost never works with the Japanese. They look for arguments based on feelings and sentiment rather than logic. As a senior executive of a large American subsidiary in Japan pointed out, ". . . decisions are based on emotional concepts, and if you appeal to that first, then you can get established on a friendly basis. Selling is not only a matter of selling the product; it is a matter of psychology and philosophy." Remember that the Japanese do not perceive emotional and sensitive businessmen as soft. An appeal to sentiment is not the same as being sentimental.

The same principle holds true for determining our approaches to right and wrong. According to Michael K. Young, associate professor of law at Columbia's Center for Japanese Legal Studies, "Americans emphasize somewhat abstract notions of right and wrong, duty and obligation. They ask, what is right? My duty? And yours? The Japanese," he continues, "emphasize the effect of any act on personal relations and ask what its impact will be on the long-term relationship between the parties involved."

Japanese commercials are wonderful examples of how the "soft," nonlogical argument sells products. An ad for a trash compactor shows a deluge of tin cans dropping from swollen rain clouds over Tokyo. And that is the entire message. An ad for an audio cassette depicts thousands of cassettes standing up domino-fashion in the most intricate and clever design imaginable. They start collapsing, running their course in myriad directions and geometric designs, until finally the last one quietly and gracefully plops into the cassette player, the lid shuts, and the music plays. In an ad for a flexible desk lamp, the lamp's flexibility is shown by tracking a fly buzzing around the room, keeping it in the beam of light, zapping it dead like a Star Wars laser gun. Then a miniature ambulance arrives to remove the dead fly. The point behind these soft-touch, affective commercials might be missed by American viewers, who look for the fast sell, the comparison of a product with its competitors, or how a product ranks in scientific tests or nationwide surveys. But for the Japanese viewer, the fun, the emotions engaged, the sense of whimsy are more convincing arguments for buying a product than the hard sell.

Personal Encounters of an Oriental Kind

Business success often hinges on one's ability to initiate and maintain good personal relations. With the Japanese, these relationships are built on the intricate foundations of correct order and propriety. In important matters as well as trivial ones, the Japanese have a sense of propriety and good order based upon centuries of social custom. The challenge for Americans is to know the tacit and subtle rules behind this propriety and then use them as strategies to meet their company's goals. Decision-making, group-think, and the need for the Japanese to save face in front of others are all significant aspects of Japanese behavior where proper conduct can make or break a deal.

The Japanese take great pains to appear polite and will go to great lengths to spare you pain. A Japanese business associate whom I knew well and worked with over a good period of time received a phone call that his father had just died. When I asked him if there was anything I could do, his response set me back. He smiled and began to laugh hysterically. Dismayed and confused, I asked a mutual friend of ours what had happened. I felt as if I had done something very wrong. Later I found out that my friend was simply trying to avoid involving me in his crisis. What I had stumbled upon was the fact that the Japanese have an intricate system of social indebtedness that covers who owes what, and how much, and to whom. If I expressed my sorrow and offered him help, then he would have felt that at some later date he would have to repay me.

Much of the surface politeness in interpersonal relationships reflects the Japanese concern with maintaining harmony. Never make the fatal error of mistaking politeness for friendship. Americans may find these two hard to differentiate. Furthermore, politeness is no guarantee that the Japanese will do business. The reverse of this is true, however: no business will take place without polite personal relationships between the parties involved.

While politeness is a necessity to oil the social machinery between companies, it is never a sign of friendship or a guarantee of the particular interpersonal relationship on which business deals are concluded. Yet from the Oriental perspective, a good business relationship must be founded upon a healthy personal relationship that has had the proper time to be nurtured and grow. The Japanese have a word for this, *nemawashi*—the watering of roots, the nurturing of a plant so that it will become sturdy and healthy.

Coffee for Me, Tea for You, Sushi for Two

Getting to know the Japanese is no easy task and is made no easier during working hours when they find it difficult to relax and open up to you. The best and often only way to get them to unwind and open up to you is after 5:00 p.m. and then only out of the office in some neutral territory, like a bar or a sushi restaurant. Even your home may be off-bounds for entertainment purposes. The Japanese prefer to be out on the town to really relax. And if they invite your wife along, politely refuse or make some excuse for her, because they prefer it that way. Their invitation was probably just a formality!

Many Americans are still overwhelmed by the Japanese tradition of lavish entertaining and long nights on the town, the style especially popular during the 1970s. In 1981 Japanese corporations spent $13.5 billion on entertainment for their clients. That's $37 million every day. The Japanese as a group are probably unmatched anywhere in the world when it comes to entertainment as a business expense. So when it is your turn to entertain your Japanese business associates, keep in mind their social expertise. You don't necessarily have to trip the light fantastic in order to impress the Japanese, but they will expect to be shown a good time with dinner and drinks if it is evening, or perhaps a Yankee baseball game, a round of golf, or an old-fashioned picnic on the weekend.

Lunch as a means of entertainment is not a good idea. The Japanese usually take short lunch breaks, and often these are in the company cafeteria. It's not uncommon for many to work right through lunch and have a light sushi or tempura snack sent in from the local Japanese restaurant. The Japanese prefer not to interrupt the workday, but some Westernized Japanese are becoming accustomed to the notion of the Western-style "working lunch" where informal yet important business is conducted during the meal.

Whether in the States or in Japan, if you are the one doing the entertaining, be careful to choose a restaurant that won't cause the Japanese embarrassment or discomfort. The senior vice-president of a large American advertising agency thought he would make a good impression on one of his Japanese clients by taking him to a popular Tex-Mex restaurant that had the local monopoly on "hot." In order to save face, Mr. Miyamoto politely consumed the chimichanga and refried beans with hot sauce ordered for him by his American host. With that, the day was shot. The poor Japanese spent the next three hours after lunch running to the men's room to examine the condition of his tongue, trying to decide whether medical help would be needed to keep it attached to his mouth! Remember that the Japanese basic diet is grains, vegetables, and fish, and they generally shy away from hot and spicy foods. This doesn't mean that you must go to a Japanese restaurant or sushi bar. But unless you know for a fact that your guests like a particular type of ethnic food, stick to rather basic restaurants with a wide selection of dishes. Also, the Japanese are accustomed to very tender and small portions of beef and can be caught off guard when presented with a well-done two-pound T-bone steak.

It is perfectly acceptable for you to order for your guests, especially if they aren't familiar with the menu or the names of certain domestic dishes, or the cute local-color names like "Barnyard Jed's Down-Home Special." And like all guests, they will be exceptionally impressed if you pick up the bill, but you must be quick. From their point of view, it is a mark of good manners to swipe the bill off the table before the host can get it.

Another entertainment hazard concerns excessive drunkenness. While it is true that the Japanese like a night on the town with a lot of hearty drinking, the effects can be deadly for someone imbibing foreign spirits in a foreign land. A Wall Street broker who was asked to take a newly married young trainee of a Japanese client out on the town tripped the lights from one popular New York singles bar to another. The next day he got a call from a colleague at the client company that the rookie was so drunk driving home to New Jersey that he forgot he was not in Japan where one drives on the left side of the street, hit a tree, suffered minor injuries, and was arrested by the police for drunk driving. Not an evening to kick off a prospective business relationship!

Getting Acquainted

Being sensitive to cultural differences while preserving your own integrity is one of the key factors in learning to relate with the Japanese successfully. Never call the Japanese by their first names or nicknames unless you are already on a first-name basis. If you want to personalize your friendship, add *san* to the end of the family name, as in "Sato-*san*." Also, never slap them on the back as a friendly "attaboy" gesture or throw your arm around their shoulders in a complimentary hug. While these may be acceptable gestures of friendship and encouragement here, public displays of affection are usually considered offensive by the Japanese and may confuse or even shock them.

Ironically, it is not uncommon to see one Japanese massaging the neck of another in the office around mid- or late-afternoon. However, I wouldn't advise Westerners to go around massaging Japanese necks!

What's So Funny?

Never laugh at a Japanese to his face. This is as close to personally affronting him as you can come. Joking around with the Japanese on the job is also a bad idea, especially since they probably won't understand or appreciate the American sense of humor, which tends to be broad and obvious. Japanese humor, on the other hand, is very subtle and dry and easily lost in translation. Except for those who are more Westernized, the Japanese often do not know how to accept humor in everyday situations. As far as they are concerned, seriousness is a virtue and mixing it with humor may be considered inappropriate. So when something funny happens or when a Japanese co-worker does something that tickles your funny bone, do not point it out or laugh out loud. There is a saying that in Japan the time to laugh is when everybody understands it's time to laugh.

Delivering the Word

Verbal communication is the most common tool for imparting and sharing information among the Japanese. Americans new to the Japanese business scene have expressed frustration over the Japanese not responding to written communications or queries. The Japanese prefer face-to-face dialogue. Limit written communications and telephone conversations to the bare necessities. Arrange for your meetings to be held in person and not over the phone. Unlike Americans, the Japanese are extremely cautious about what they say on the phone. Only use phone calls to handle logistics and arrange meetings, never to discuss substantive issues. On the other hand, the Japanese like and appreciate the personal touch in business relations and enjoy receiving "courtesy calls" for a chat or just to say "hello."

For the same reason, letters are probably the least effective technique for introducing yourself to a Japanese company or its director. There are exceptions to this rule. For example, U.S. subsidiaries of Japanese companies or even American subsidiaries in Japan are accustomed to responding to written communications. The rule of thumb, though, is that if your contact is Japanese, try to use a go-between to make the initial introduction.

When speaking to a Japanese who understands a little English, speak slowly and enunciate your words clearly. Avoid idiomatic expressions like "ballpark figures," "the bottom line," and "that's a lot of baloney." If you have any doubts about whether the Japanese understood what you said, repeat yourself. Be specific and use analogies to help illustrate your main points. Also, it isn't a bad idea to confirm later in writing, perhaps in a conference report, the main points of agreement reached during the discussion.

Being of Service

One of the most vital elements of Japanese propriety is the notion of being of service. The Japanese are great pleasers and will go out of their way to put the little touches on their transactions that Westerners often find superfluous. Gift-giving is one of these niceties that you may want to incorporate into your own business style. It is customary to give gifts to your clients and even your customers in Japan as a token of your appreciation for their long-term relationship with you. There are two gift-giving periods in Japan, the middle of July and December, during which times company bonuses are also awarded.

While it is not mandatory that you give gifts during these seasons to your Japanese employees in this country, it can go a long way in keeping your relationships on an even keel. As long as you specify that you are giving the gift as a token of your appreciation for their business, work, or service, it will not be interpreted as a bribe (as the Japanese might suspect you of, knowing the role that gift-giving has in American business and politics!). Good gift suggestions include liquor, theater tickets, dinners, even reasonably priced consumer gadgets.

When it comes to being of service and performing friendly courtesies, don't overlook after-sales customer service. The Japanese take great pride in and attach exceptional importance to this. As two Americans living in Japan relate: "Last summer our lawnmower was malfunctioning. Time and again we returned it to the shop where we had purchased it. Eventually, in exasperation, we took it back and angrily told the sales clerks that we would never again buy the company's products. The shop assistants were overcome with remorse. We left the lawnmower to be repaired yet again, and carried on with various chores in town. By the time we got home the lawnmower had been repaired and returned. And to show their penitence, the repairmen had mowed the lawn for us!"

Attention to detail is almost a fanatical habit with the Japanese. Acting as a troubleshooter, taking care of special favors, or providing highly valued competitive or strategic information will go a long way toward cementing your relationship with them. Advertising and public relations firms with Japanese clients can attest to the need to perform services above and beyond the call of duty. Comparable Japanese agencies are extremely service-oriented and will frequently perform "extra" duties such as collecting competitive marketing or sales information.

The Japanese term "plus alpha" says it all. To keep a competitive edge on other companies, you must do something extra, something free, something the customer does not normally require but still expects from you. And something with no strings attached.

Don't expect to be complimented or patted on the back for a job well done. Being as group-oriented as they are, the Japanese don't favor singling out an individual in the group and rewarding him or her for outstanding work. The group or section takes the reward, and should you single out one worker for acknowledgment, you may upset that person's humble composure. Avoid giving awards for outstanding achievement or instituting an incentive program for individual Japanese employees, unless they are thoroughly Westernized or work for an American company.

Respecting Status

Propriety pops its head up in many places, but in none more obviously than the area of status. Japan has an extremely status-conscious culture, and in some ways this can work to your advantage. The virtue of a society with clear-cut notions of status is that one always knows where he or she belongs, what is expected, what is right and proper behavior, what is improper. It may take you a while to learn the various taboos, but once you know them, you need not worry about what is expected of you in social and business situations.

For the neophyte, however, the question of status can be perplexing because you will not know all the rules until you become acquainted with the Japanese, but in order to become acquainted with them, you need to observe the proper rules. Sound like Catch -22? It is. The Japanese are a wary people when encountering strangers and a strict code of conduct governs those first meetings with potential business associates.

Jack Seward, author and Japanophile, relates the story of an American who engaged his Japanese neighbor to introduce him to a company with which he hoped to do business, not realizing that the neighbor's position with the company was far below that of company representatives he would have to deal with. He found that it took him several weeks longer to finally work his way up to the person who could make the arrangements to fully consider the American's services for the firm. And to further compound the breach of etiquette, the company felt obliged to retain the go-between in all their later transactions with the American even though the Japanese involved felt uncomfortable that someone of lower status was sitting in on discussions that did not directly concern him. He was even required to attend conferences and evening entertainments with higher-ups who naturally considered him out of place.[2] So the moral of the story is to choose your go-between carefully, keeping your eye on the status considerations involved.

If you are looking to establish an office in Japan, you may find that hiring a top-level Japanese executive is essential for the venture to succeed. This executive can serve the role of go-between, bridging the yawning gulf that separates Japanese and American business cultures while also serving as an invaluable resource in new market development. But more on the go-between later.

Business Cards and Job Titles

Getting yourself in the front door can take time, even years. Be patient. But when you have successfully negotiated all the arrangements through your go-between, be sure to have your business cards, or *meishi*, handy. A card for everyone on your team is a must. Your calling card immediately codifies for the Japanese who you are, where you work, and your specific status. Knowing these things about you indicates to them how to deal with you, how much respect to show, what to expect back from you, and who in their company is your counterpart. You might think that such matters can wait or will evolve naturally from personal contact, but the Japanese are hesitant even to initiate personal contact without knowing who you are, what authority you have, how much respect you command.

If possible, have your card printed in both Japanese and English, and make sure not to hand it over upside down. Also, remember that English job titles don't necessarily translate well into Japanese titles, so make sure your title aptly describes your responsibilities. If, after establishing a relationship with a Japanese company, the Japanese discover that your job title denotes a greater responsibility than you actually have, they may interpret this as a breach of business etiquette and suffer unnecessary guilt for having "mistreated" you earlier on.

Discovering a New Sense of Time

Status-conscious cultures demand much patience from the outsider. Business transactions take longer because of the imposed rituals that preserve and oil the machinery of personal relations. Your patience will most likely reap rewards. Fortunately the Japanese do not do everything slowly. There is a "slow, slow, fast, fast" dynamic operating in Japanese business. While they are initially slow in making decisions and getting the ball rolling, when it rolls, it rolls quickly. Their implementation of decisions is swift and usually surprises Americans who are used to the opposite: quick decisions but considerable foot-dragging to get the decision into operation. You may have to develop a new sense of time and exert considerable patience when the Japanese ask incessant questions that seem irrelevant to you. Remember that for them to make decisions they must have answers to help them make the "right" or "best" decisions. Give them as much time as they seem to think they need, rather than what you think they need. This difference in time may make all the difference in the world, both in the present negotiation and in future ones. Remember that time is relative, and you are each working on a different concept of time.

Patience can and will produce results. To the Japanese, a patient person has the sweet smell of success; an impatient person reeks of disaster. Too often the American businessman races to the quarterly bottom line and makes present decisions based on near-future prospects. The Japanese, with an eye on the long-term results, find this tactic foolish and reckless. The Japanese perceive impatience as a serious weakness. They are wary of trusting someone as a business partner who cannot wait patiently for long-term results. As one Japanese businessman said, "You Americans have a terrible weakness [impatience], and we Japanese know it and exploit it every chance we get."

New on the Job

The need to bide your time also holds true if you are hired to work for a Japanese company. Allow sufficient time to acclimate yourself to the foreign setting either here or abroad. Keep a low profile at first, and be prepared to put in long hours. The Japanese are forever amused by the American habit of leaving the office at five o'clock. Long hours are a sign of devotion to the company, and they will stay at their desks even after quitting time if the boss is still around. They may have nothing to do but read the newspaper or play chess, but they won't leave until the boss does. It would be considered a sign of insubordination and bad faith. To the Japanese, work always comes first and foremost.

Furthermore, don't expect to be given a detailed job description when joining a Japanese company. As we saw with the new recruits at Mitsubishi, Japanese managers will expect you to catch on with time. A recently recruited marketing assistant for a Japanese company, hired away from IBM, claimed it took two years of "winging it" because his Japanese supervisors always became irritated by his requests for job definitions. Be patient. Your duties will become apparent eventually, and the period of searching and wondering what you're there for may offer you opportunities to learn about the company, its people, and the way they do business.

A danger you, like many Westerners, may fall into when doing business with the Japanese is the "know-it-all" syndrome. A modicum of success can give people the impression that they have mastered the intricacies of Japanese etiquette. This experience, coupled with long days, even weeks, of patiently waiting for results, can delude you into thinking that at last you have arrived, when in reality you're still at the gate. Don't jump the gun. Don't imagine you are safely entrenched in the Japanese business community too easily. You may still have a long way to go, and you may still have setbacks and delays you didn't plan on.

Preserving Harmony

The more you become adept at the dynamics of Japanese business culture, the more you will see that much of the strict code of conduct, developed over centuries of feudal life and now expertly adapted to the corporate life, has one main goal: preserving harmony. The Land of the Rising Sun has, in spite of occasional outbursts of international militarism, created a society reflective of the peaceful calm the dawn suggests. An island society in which the citizenry spend most of their lives working in groups, the Japanese have devised a system of etiquette to maintain the delicate harmony required of close group activity. The brusque, everyone-for-themselves attitude, so typical of American democracy, has to a large extent been avoided by the Japanese brand of democratic institutions.

Tatemae and *Honne*

Two key terms for understanding the Japanese concept of harmony are *tatemae*, which is form, and *honne*, which means substance. Form and substance, two concepts well known in the West, are always assumed by us to go hand in hand. Or let's say hand in glove, where the glove is the *tatemae* (form) and the hand is the *honne* (substance). The average Westerner expects form and substance to coincide in sincere social relations. If not, something looks deceitful, duplicitous, fishy. When we project an outward appearance of agreement or concern or interest (form) while inside harboring disagreement, lack of concern, or disinterest (substance), it usually makes us appear two-faced or forked-tongued, as American Indians have pointed out on enough occasions. Yet we do it, and even justify it to ourselves. When others do it to us, however, we feel used, we distrust them, we accuse them of conniving for their own gain.

The extent to which the Japanese will go to save face and preserve harmony can verge on the comically absurd. A friend comes to visit and finds a husband and wife in the midst of the biggest fight of their lives. Pots, pans, and angry words are being thrown back and forth between the two. When the door opens, it's obvious that it is an inopportune moment for visitors, as a dish goes whizzing past the friend's head. Immediately he takes stock of the situation, bows deeply (for *tatemae*'s sake and to duck a low-flying pot), and says, "I apologize for intruding during your housecleaning. It is my fault that I did not consider that night time is the best time to straighten one's house; not that yours needed straightening. It is undoubtedly one of the neatest houses I have ever visited, and now it will be more so. Please excuse my intrusion." He bows and exits.

A bit farfetched, perhaps, but all the elements of *tatemae* are there. The trespassing friend, in order to spare his married friends any embarrassment, pretended to read their squabble as housecleaning and took the onus of intrusion upon himself even though he had been invited. Certainly no one was fooled, but all were grateful and pretended that the fellow really did stumble into their housecleaning chores.

It is important, therefore, for Westerners to understand that the Japanese, especially in the process of negotiating or in any group setting, find it perfectly legitimate and ethical to work both sides of the street at the same time, as it were, saying one thing for the sake of form (*tatemae*), to preserve harmony, while at the same time holding certain reservations, doubts, exceptions to what one is saying (*honne*). Juggling *tatemae* and *honne* is one of the most effective of the Japanese tactics in bargaining and negotiating. What's more, it is perfectly acceptable to the Japanese to allow two contradictory points of view to exist simultaneously in the name of preserving harmony. Major contradictory positions can be reconciled later behind the scenes where the losing side can save face.

Saving Face

No matter what you think or feel about the American counterparts of *tatemae* and *honne*, to the Japanese they will appear as acceptable, legitimate maneuvers to preserve group harmony even at the expense of what Westerners would call logic or common sense. Learn to read your Japanese associates in these terms, and allow them their idiosyncratic yet justifiable need to save face. The need to save face determines many essential rules of business etiquette. Here are some you should never forget:

• Never confront the Japanese with a direct charge or accusation. This will only serve to embarrass them and will surely lead to the demise of your relationship. Rather you should suggest what you have in mind *indirectly* or in such a manner that the Japanese can bring the ticklish topic up themselves. Call the others' attention to the matter and suggest that they may want to consider it further later on when they are alone.

• Never ask a Japanese person a question that he or she may not be able to answer. Only ask a direct question if you are absolutely positive that it can be responded to adequately. The Japanese often like to know your questions ahead of time in order that they may have sufficient time to consult the group and consider all the alternatives and possibilities. Failure to be prepared can lead to loss of face.

• Use a go-between to communicate unpleasant or unfortunate matters, regardless of where the fault lies. The go-between can often be the same person who originally introduced you or one who is familiar and on good terms with both parties.

• Never communicate outright refusal or rejection to the Japanese. Always suggest that you will consider the matter further; if you later have to say no to some proposal, always present your reasons in a clear, coherent, and nonthreatening manner. The Japanese have no provision within their language for categorically refusing or saying no. Americans find this especially disorienting and must learn to read the subtle cues in order to know when the Japanese have in fact said no. Common signs of a negative response are an unwillingness to be specific, faltering in speech, and a hesitancy in response.

Conclusion

Endless discussion, ritual face-saving, talking around issues, beating around the bush—all of these are important elements in the Japanese code of conduct, a code based primarily on the desire to preserve harmony. Coming to agreement with the Japanese is a process that will fail if the conditions for group harmony are shattered, and how easily that can be done by Americans who are blind to the demands of Japanese conduct! If the Japanese perceive your behavior as a threat to their sense of harmony, they will regard you as an unreliable business partner, one in whom they cannot place their trust and confidence; and trusting your company will never replace the trust the Japanese must first have in you. Without sacrificing your own personal and professional integrity, you must become one with them, rather than one of them, and in so doing, lay the foundation for a rewarding business relationship.

CHAPTER 5

Bargaining and Negotiation: New Ways to Get What You Want

FACT: according to an inside source in the U.S. Department of Commerce, for every successful Japanese-American negotiation there are twenty-five failures. Surely, then, both the Japanese and Americans must be among the world's worst and least effective negotiators. You may also wonder why there are proportionately so few business discussions that result in terms of agreement acceptable to both sides. Is the current generation of American businessmen ignorant of the art of negotiating? Hardly. Business schools and graduate programs offer outstanding courses in negotiating. Popular best-sellers on how to negotiate have dealt with every conceivable aspect of the topic. So why do well-trained Americans suddenly become dysfunctional when they sit down at a table across from a Japanese negotiating team?

On his 1983 visit to Washington, Prime Minister Yasuhiro Nakasone placed the blame for many of the failures between the two nations on the fact that American businessmen do not understand Japanese businessmen. An accurate perception, but only half the story. Every failed negotiation is a failure on both sides. According to the managing director of a major Japanese auto company who has had a great deal of experience with Western business people, many negotiating teams are like "two trains hurtling down parallel tracks, both headed in the same direction. One train represents the Western way of looking at things and the other train symbolizes the Japanese way of seeing things. A Westerner might say, 'Ah well, at least they're running alongside one another with many things in common; better parallel lines of thought than divergent.' But a Japanese would say, 'Unfortunately, despite all the things in common between the two locomotives, they are destined to continue forever alongside one another without ever meeting.' These two valid points of view seem contradictory, and it is this type of contradiction which causes so much misunderstanding among Japanese and other businessmen. . . . It's really just a way of looking at things and appreciating the other man's point of view."

Failures are often preordained because of a basic Western ignorance of how the Japanese operate as a negotiating team. Many Westerners feel confident that they can deal with the Japanese by being open and direct, an approach that frequently works in the West. "Get that Japanese company on the phone. I've got a deal for them. Put me through to their president. No, better yet, I want to talk to the chairman." If that's your style, and variations of it are popular and effective in the U.S., you should know that it is not the Japanese style. Going straight to the top and damning the torpedoes is the quickest way to sink whatever chances you had for a successful business transaction.

Style: Non-negotiable

Before we look at the negotiating process itself, let's take a look at the style of negotiating that has proved successful in dealing with the Japanese. You will recognize some of the elements of style from the preceding chapters on "illusions" and "etiquette," but a quick review will help you understand what actually contributes to success or failure around the negotiating table.

Politeness with a Sword

Foremost is the necessity to be polite or at least appear polite. Coming from a formal and status-conscious society, the Japanese expect business negotiations to reflect the propriety and good order they demand in other areas. Yet beneath the superficial politeness of the Japanese negotiators is their true style of negotiating, which is typically a ruthless "we win, you lose" strategy. You might think that the Japanese with their veneer of politeness and their own desire to save face and come to consensual decisions would favor the win-win style of negotiating. But they don't. Negotiating for the Japanese is a win-lose struggle. The desired aim is to win while maintaining the polite formalities without which the negotiating process will fail.

Here are some specific ways to maintain an atmosphere of politeness:

• Smile always, even when it hurts.
• Be humble and good-natured.
• Develop a calm, open, nonthreatening attitude.
• Avoid sounding egotistical.
• Be emotionally sensitive, remembering that the Japanese are persuaded by affective arguments, not logical ones. Be aware of their personal feelings.
• While being sensitive to their feelings, avoid flattery and saccharine compliments. Most of these sound hollow anyway.
• Be careful not to criticize the Japanese openly. They will feel insecure if they lose face in front of their colleagues and you. Never make comments that judge the Japanese or their actions. "You want us to do what? You're crazy! Oh, come on, do you think we're fools?" Judgmental statements like these will surely humiliate your opponents and bring the session to an icy halt.
• Refrain from criticizing either the Japanese or American government. The Japanese may consider it a breach of etiquette to use the government as a whipping boy, so hold your comments even if you had intended them jokingly. The humor will undoubtedly be lost in the translation.
• Do not confront the Japanese or catch them off guard no matter what you have read about winning through intimidation. They usually have no immediate response to handle open challenges. They are uncomfortable ad-libbing excuses or alibis, and will be embarrassed by your comments as well as by their failure to respond. If something occurs that disturbs you or needs clarification, present it informally outside

of the negotiating session. If it's a particularly touchy issue, have your go-between present it to them. In this way you will be sure to get a response and the Japanese will appreciate your sensitivity and tact.

• Apologize for everything, especially the things that you are not in the least sorry for. It is a Japanese custom to assume fault where no fault is visible. For example, it is not uncommon for a Japanese to find a wallet in the street and return it to its owner and apologize for not having brought it sooner The Japanese frequently note how seldom we say, "I'm sorry," a phrase as automatic for them as "Have a nice day" is for some of us. In addition, realize that apologies from your opponents may not run very deep either. Chances are that the one apologizing isn't the least bit sorry.

• Do not assume that unexplained or "inscrutable" behavior is a sign of deception or trickery. It is a natural inclination to be suspicious of one's opponent in a negotiating session, and remember that the possibility of illusions is infinitely greater between American and Japanese simply because of their vastly different culture backgrounds. So give the Japanese the benefit of the doubt and trust that they are being sincere with you.

• On the other hand, don't mistake politeness for friendship. Politeness is a cultural *style*, not an indication of personal *feelings*.

In addition to these guidelines, remember that your style of negotiating will have to accommodate the Japanese use of *honne* and *tatemae*. Takahiro Nikano, a Japan specialist at the New York State Department of Commerce, warns that a party who doesn't understand the core issues of a business transaction, i.e., *honne*, will be the loser. The Japanese, he continues, like "room to play [in a negotiation] without actually cheating." In other words, they know how to artfully manipulate the substance of the issues at hand and the formality with which they deal with those issues. We'll see later how this comes into play in the actual negotiation process.

Preliminaries: The Prebargaining Stages

The preliminary phase is a critical element of the negotiating process. The premeeting activities lay the groundwork for what follows, and if managed properly, with forethought and shrewdness, can make the actual negotiating itself much more satisfactory for you. Mistakes made during the prebargaining phase can often prove destructive later on.

The Go-Between

When you are ready to approach your target Japanese company with your proposal, you should always attempt to use a go-between. Do not confront the company yourself. The Japanese do not feel comfortable with the direct, hard-sell approach. Consequently, a third party, familiar and respected by both the Japanese and your company, may be far more effective in breaking down the initial barriers. Who should your go-between be?

• It should probably be a man. The Japanese company is a male-dominated institution and a woman serving as a go-between would be considered out of place.

• The go-between should be thoroughly knowledgeable about your company, your product and/or service, and the deal you intend to propose.

• The go-between should be a third party. Preferably not someone from your company nor the Japanese company, but someone familiar to both and trusted by the Japanese. When making a selection of a go-between, consider someone from a reputable trading company, a trading agent, a representative of another company that the Japanese have done business with, a bank officer, or a member of an industrial or trade association whom the Japanese respect.

• The go-between should be of a status equal to the personnel with whom he will have to deal. Someone too high or too low will create social and possible political tensions either at the start or certainly later on when the go-between will attend social and entertainment functions.

In general, the go-between should approach someone on the middle-management level. By no means should he go to the top. Decisions begin on the lower to middle levels in Japanese firms and work their way up. Even the decision to meet with an American company to negotiate a business deal begins in the middle echelons, not the top. For this reason, the go-between should present the idea to someone in middle management who will then discuss the idea with his colleagues and report to his supervisor. Your offer to negotiate will then begin its slow crawl to the level on which the actual negotiating takes place.

The go-between's initial contact should always be in person. Letters and phone calls usually will not do. Also, it is best if the go-between suggests some neutral ground, such as a hotel, on which to meet.

RSVP Japanese-Style

Once the invitation has been made, sit back and wait. Let the Japanese take all the time they need to react to your "feeler." Your best ploy is to give them the impression that you have all the time in the world. Impetuosity and impatience are signs of weakness to them. During this period, the Japanese will find out who you are through their own business information network. They always want to thoroughly know who they will be dealing with before they actually meet you. Your inclination might be to say, "Let's get together and see who these people are." But their approach is to say, "Let's see who these people are and then get together." The Japanese will check your recommendations and references. These are important. Japanese companies share a lot of information with each other about foreign companies they deal with, so it will take time for them to track down your record and evaluate it to their satisfaction. They will even want to know what other companies you do business with. For them, *whom* you do business with is as important as *how* you do business.

During this time it is a good idea for you to do some study yourself. Presumably you have already done enough to know that you want to do business with this particular company. But remember that information is power, especially at the negotiating table, so learn all you can from third parties. It is valuable to know the Japanese company's financial situation, its corporate needs and priorities, power structure, assets and liabilities, other deals in progress (if possible), and even what other companies it has refused to do business with and why. As the Japanese get closer to agreeing to meet with you, try to find out from third parties or someone in the company who the individuals are that you will be dealing with and learn all you can about them.

When a signal is given, most likely through the go-between, that the "getting to know you" stage is over, they will instruct their contact to invite you or a delegation from your company to present your offer. This stage is not the time to spill the beans. Rather, a broad outline of your objectives should be presented to the Japanese in person. This outline, which might serve as a rough agenda for the first actual negotiating session, should be delivered verbally and not put in writing. Remember that a verbal commitment is as sacred to the Japanese as a written commitment is to Westerners. Be extremely careful, therefore, about what you say. If you sound like you are pledging yourself to something, they will remember it and remind you of it later.

The Initial Get-Together

Your first meetings with the Japanese will most likely be informal situations, like dinners and quasi-social gatherings, where they will take your pulse and do a face-to-face reading of your personality and trustworthiness. These get-togethers always precede the official consent to sit down and negotiate, so don't be surprised if the Japanese seem to feint and poke around during this stage. Your best response is to couch what you say with statements like, "That is an interesting proposal; we'll have to consider it further" or "I'm not prepared to respond to that issue right now, but perhaps at some future point we can discuss it further." Then ask for another Chivas on the rocks.

If pressed, make sure that any prebargaining ground rules are conditional to subsequent phases of negotiating. Don't give anything up unless you get something in return. If you show them your quid, make them show you their quo. But temper your requests with the realization that at this point the Japanese most likely do not have clear objectives. It is their style not to have complete understanding of everything they hope to get out of the business relationship you are proposing to create with them. Be prepared for replies that sound evasive. If the Japanese sound unsure of themselves in these preliminary sessions, it is because they probably *are* unsure of themselves.

The Japanese strongly feel that the first party to make a unilateral concession is the weaker of the two. Most Westerners often make minor, trivial concessions to one another as a show of good faith. This tactic, however, is an error in dealing with the Japanese. They would view a concession, such as in price or delivery terms, as an admission that you needed them more than they needed you. The only other explanation that would occur to them for your having made concessions so early and so easily was that you were insincere or inconsistent, two characteristics that can convince the Japanese not to do business with you. It is better to arrange things so that the first concessions are simultaneous. Hold out for this to occur or cause it to occur at an opportune moment. You need not be concerned that the Japanese will see you as intransigent or stubborn. Rather, they will see you as consistent in your strategy and will respect you more for it.

Now for the bad news. Once the Japanese have agreed to enter into serious negotiations with you, plan to set up permanent camp. It will take a long time. Be prepared to stay in negotiations a good five to six times longer than you would normally expect when negotiating the same type of business arrangement with another American company. Typical Japanese-American negotiations will try your staying power, and only the long-suffering will survive.

The Negotiating Team

Who should be on your team? How many negotiators will you need? Should there be specialists among your negotiators? These and other such questions are of vital concern to the success of the bargaining process.

Power-Wielders and Power-Welders

Chief executive officers and other senior officials usually are not the best people to enter the negotiations at the early stages. If the ultimate decision needs their participation, they will enter later. People who do not have the ultimate authority to go straight to the bottom line can weld a deal together more easily and more convincingly than the top man. The president of your company or the CEO has too much authority for early sessions where it is important to give and take, discuss conditions and requirements, piece together proposals, and be ready to compromise.

Most important is to have a good balance between both teams as regards the level of authority. The Japanese, as well as most Americans, prefer negotiating with people on their own level of status. If one team is top-heavy with individuals who exercise more authority and influence in their company than do the individuals on the opposing team, that inequality can negatively affect the course of the discussions.

So there are two basic questions you should ask about your opponents: What authority do they have? What decisions can they make? Then select your negotiators accordingly.

If you hire a professional negotiator for your company, it

should be someone the Japanese are familiar with and trust. He should also be thoroughly briefed on your own company, the deal being negotiated, and the individual Japanese with whom he will bargain.

The number of individuals to select for your team is always a problem. No matter how many people you choose, the Japanese will show up with more. Expect to be outnumbered. Don't try to surreptitiously add more over the course of the negotiations. The Japanese will match you. Eventually you'll have to move the negotiations to a football stadium. The Japanese like to have a lot of people on their side for several reasons. One is obviously the psychological effect: having a larger army unnerves the opposition. But a less devious reason than intimidation is that the Japanese decision-making process requires the input of employees on various levels and from various departments. The more people involved in the negotiating process, the easier it will be later when the principals making the decision have to reach a consensus.

The Interpreter

While many Japanese subsidiaries have an army of English-speaking personnel, the detailed discussion in a negotiation may still require professional translators. Many American companies make the mistake of assuming that the Japanese translator is all that is needed. Smooth negotiations require two translators, one on each side. Be sure the translator is briefed thoroughly on the business under discussion because a well-informed interpreter can also be used as a sounding board and adviser during those moments in the bargaining when you feel your next move depends on how your opponents are reacting to the discussion so far. A bilingual member of your team will be able to read the opposition much more accurately than those of you who cannot distinguish subtle nuances in expression and interpret the connotations of what is being said in Japanese. Further instructions on how to use the translator are given later in this chapter.

Who Not to Include

If at all possible, exclude lawyers, accountants, and other professional consultants from your negotiating team. The Japanese will not have them on theirs. Most Japanese have an abiding mistrust of lawyers and perceive those who depend on them for counsel before each move as untrustworthy. In their minds, lawyers are experts at deception (a view not totally unheard of in the West!) and if you give the impression that you are relying on them before making decisions, the Japanese will conclude that you are more concerned with the "fine print" than with the substance of the discussions. So if you can get by without having a lawyer as a principal negotiator, do so. A lawyer and, to a lesser degree, an accountant and a consultant, will retard progress.

One last word about the negotiators. Don't change negotiators in midstream. Doing so denotes inconsistency, weakness, insincerity; and the Japanese temperament being what it is, the other side will feel the need to return to stage one: getting to know you. You never want to return to stage one!

Making Your Presentation

Unlike the hard, fast sell typical of American negotiations, your presentation to the Japanese must be low-keyed and avoid extravagant claims. Recall how the American team for Videomart got off on the wrong foot by the old American hard, fast sell. You must take the opposite approach. Even when you first enter the room and shake hands, do not use a hard, firm grip and a lot of macho arm-pumping. This is a delicate, formal Japanese ceremony, not a John Wayne movie. Be polite, shake hands gently, and don't call the Japanese by their first names.

The Purpose—and the Real Purpose

You must be constantly aware during your presentation that it serves two purposes: to introduce your product or service to the Japanese team and to allow the Japanese to size your team up. No matter whether individuals on your team have already met the Japanese, they are still evaluating your personalities and judging character. In fact, they aren't really that interested in your product at this point. They are more concerned about commitment to that product, how reliable you will be in servicing the product, and what kind of personal commitment you are making to them, the Japanese company. Be reminded that the Japanese are very emotional people and that in the early stages of negotiation they are testing their unwritten code of trust, discovering how "civil" you will be both now and in future dealings with their personnel.

Is Anyone Over There Listening?

A question usually arises with Americans as to which member or members of the Japanese team carry the most clout and to whom they should aim their pitch. This is a tricky issue. You may not be able to tell, especially during the presentation, when the Japanese may all be sitting there glassy-eyed and stone-faced. First, do not assume that the Japanese are fully knowledgeable about you, your company, or the issues. It's true they've done their homework and come well-prepped as a team. But individually, not everyone will be familiar with all the issues involved. Talk to everyone, not just the oldest or the designated leader. On account of the Japanese practice of job rotation, there may be heads of departments on the team who have just recently assumed their positions. Mere titles do not indicate how long an individual has been in a position or how much experience he has. Even the designated leader may not be fully briefed and will rely on subordinates off and on during the negotiations for information and advice. It is part of the Japanese decision-making methodology to seek out everyone's opinion. So exclude no one in your presentation because, as a senior executive at Sony Corporation of America advises, it's "hard to tell who really has power in a Japanese company."

The Japanese utilize long moments of silence during meetings, silence that sometimes unnerves Americans. Be ready to wait patiently and politely during these times when the Japanese are thinking, reflecting, planning what to say next. The Americans' tendency is to talk nonstop until their point is made—and how important it is to make our point! As a rule, we are uncomfortable being with someone who is not talking (or listening!) to us. We are not predisposed to share moments of silence with professional associates.

Sometimes you may notice that one of the Japanese at a meeting falls asleep in the middle of your big presentation. By Western standards, this is not only impolite and rude, it also offends our sense of professionalism. But in the group-oriented dynamics of Japanese transactions, a brief catnap by one member of the team will not stymie the business at hand. Never assume that the Japanese falls asleep because what you are saying is boring or not worth listening to. It probably has nothing to do with what you are saying. It's most likely due to the fact that he's tired from having to deal through translators or conduct business in a language that does not come easy for him. It is not a breach of etiquette to drift off in a business meeting.

Friendly Persuasion

Your strategy during the presentation should be persuasion, not pressure—persuasion that your company can meet the needs and desires of the Japanese company. How to do this? Be clear and show evidence. Most of all, do not pressure them or make them feel foolish should they not accept your offer. High-pressured tactics are considered a sign of insincerity.

A true mark of sincerity is to have in print evidence for the claims you make about your company, its product, its past record of satisfying customers and dealing equitably with partner-companies. Visual aids are also appreciated. If possible, have printed hand-outs translated into Japanese. Have enough copies for everyone and let them keep the copies when the meeting breaks up. This includes copies of charts and film strips.

When it comes time for the Japanese to respond to your presentation, be ready for a barrage of questions, some seemingly irrelevant and out of place at the moment. You may think that you have already answered the majority of their questions in your initial presentation, but when it comes to communicating with the Japanese, it never hurts to repeat yourself. One American executive at Panasonic claims that he usually adds at least one half hour to all his presentations to the Japanese to allow for the "repeat" questions. Be patient and receptive to all of them and answer them to the best of your ability. And watch out for what might seem to you like an unreasonably extreme initial position for them to take right off the bat. People who have a win-lose style of negotiating are likely to begin with extreme initial positions. The Japanese will do so. Don't let it throw you off your guard and spark an exasperated or hostile reaction from you. Take it calmly, smile, thank them, say you're sorry (for anything), and that you will consider their "extremely interesting proposal." Then get the hell out of there!

Bargaining

Know from the beginning that the Japanese don't like the bargaining process and do not consider themselves good at it. They feel uncomfortable at the bargaining table. Americans, on the other hand, generally love a good fight. Perhaps it retains some flavor of horse-trading from the Old West. The important point is that you must tone down your bargaining tactics so that the Japanese don't feel even more ill at ease. Don't pressure them. It usually serves no purpose other than making them less sure of themselves and then they will feel the need to confer among themselves even more than normal to reach a consensus.

Is Everyone Over There Sleeping?

But the Japanese table behavior will make you feel uncomfortable, too. The Japanese can and will sit in a stone-faced silence for long periods of time. This does not signify loss of interest or disagreement with what you are saying. Nor does it indicate disagreement among the Japanese. If you are looking for physical indications that what you are saying is giving them a hard time, watch for a burst of breath through the teeth in a "zsah" sound accompanied by a loss of eye contact. This usually means that they find your point difficult to accept or that they need more time to consider it or perhaps want additional information. The stone-faced silence, the noncommittal attitude you often see during bargaining, is typical. It means they are evaluating what you are saying or that they need more time. Remember, their inclination is not to be forthcoming with any important information or commitment until they have seen the entire picture.

For this reason, they will often seem vague on certain points when you ask them direct questions. They tend not to answer until they feel they have all the information they need, and in their minds, some of that information might have to come from others in the group. The opinions, the insights, the positions of other individuals on their team is important knowledge for each one to have before he can make a definite statement about this or that. So when someone answers, "I don't know" on an issue that you know he knows something about, he is not being devious. He is probably waiting until he gets his comrades' input; "I don't know" is in fact a true statement from his point of view.

The Exchange of Power

The Japanese need as much data as possible. In spite of their ambivalence and evasiveness, they are meticulous thinkers who evaluate every scrap of evidence and information they can. They may ask for specifics about some point that you don't think is apropos at the moment or that you honestly don't have at your fingertips. For example, they may want to know engineering specifications that from your point of view have nothing to do with the point under discussion or which you believe are none of their business at the moment. Sometimes guarantees on delivery dates two or three years hence might be extremely important for them to know, dates which your company would prefer to work out later, after there is agreement on more substantive issues. Or they may ask to see copies of correspondence you just received from your home office on some point or other that came up previously. To you it is confidential material, but to the Japanese it should be shared. They don't understand how their request is a violation of privacy. In general, try to understand their questions and requests that may seem outlandish to you. Give them information whenever you can do so without jeopardizing your bargaining position.

Throughout all this give and take, the requests and counter-requests, do not lose sight of the cardinal rule in negotiating: *information is power.* It is best not to reveal too much information too easily. The more your opponent knows, the better position he is in. What you need to become adept at is fielding their questions while asking your own and trying to get definite, clear answers from them. Not an easy task! But remember that it is usually better for you to *ask* questions than for you to *answer* too many.

An Offer They Can't Refuse

In the course of every negotiation, there are many moments when one side or the other considers increasing its offer. Usually, in the West, this moves the negotiation ahead. Not always in Japan. When Americans increase an offer, the Japanese lose confidence in their sincerity. As we have seen repeatedly, sincerity and compatibility are more important to them than the lowest bid or the highest profit margin. Trust and confidence in you and your company are what seal a deal. They want to know that you will be a trustworthy partner. What you say and do at the table and the history of your proven performance are often more important than changing your offer or making them a so-called "better proposal." No matter what Don Corleone may think, there are many offers the Japanese can refuse!

The Japanese as Southern Politician

Most business meetings seem to drag on as if they were heading toward some point of no return. Meetings with the Japanese especially seem to be endless filibuster sessions. There are a couple of reasons for this and you should not worry when the meeting appears to dissolve into fruitless talk. For one thing, you should plan to do extra talking yourself (keeping in mind the needs of the translator, of course!) because the Japanese like to hear the same thing repeated in different ways. Like the long-winded storyteller of the Old South, the Japanese like analogies, extended apostrophes and parallels, and use them frequently in conversation to make a point. *Haiku* poetry, written and known by most literate Japanese, is filled with apostrophes. "No one spoke, neither the host, nor the guest, nor the white chrysanthemum." It's when you get to the white chrysanthemum that you might think the conversation is beginning to dribble. But it's not. The Japanese are always glad to hear another image so don't think that you're beating a dead horse.

Filibustering will occur on the Japanese side too. Don't become alarmed when one member drones on and on. A typical story is told by a metals trader at a large Japanese trading company who spent two days listening to a marketing presentation by one of his clients—a presentation that he painfully recalls could have been made in thirty minutes by any American firm. "But you have to learn how to tolerate the additional drudgery when negotiating with the Japanese," he concludes. Sometimes the Japanese will filibuster if they don't have a ready answer at the moment to save face with other members of the team. Or sometimes prolonged discourse is intended to provide "think time" for the other members to consider what's being discussed, formulate their thoughts, and eventually jump in to help the long-winded speaker out. All of this, of course, will seem even longer to you as you watch the conversation from both sides slowing down as it is filtered through the poor interpreter.

Beau Gestures

Most important at every stage of the bargaining is not to lose your temper or display hostility. You have to learn how to disagree without seeming disagreeable. The Japanese will not expect you to agree to everything, but they *will* expect you to keep your cool. Remember that nonverbal communication is often more telling than what you actually say— especially if you have no idea how it might be interpreted. Watch your gestures. Don't shake your finger at someone, pound on the table, or slap your fist into the palm of your hand; these movements could be interpreted as expressions of anger or hostility.

At crucial points in the negotiation sessions you may want to send "letters of understanding" to the Japanese side. These can be invaluable in lengthy negotiations that drag on for weeks and where it is important to keep both sides reminded of what has been agreed upon. For example, if you think that you have reached agreement (or even a point of disagreement) but are unsure if everyone else perceives it as you do, by all means, write up your understanding and present it to the Japanese "for clarification's sake." If you are unsure how this will be accepted, discuss it with one of the members of the Japanese negotiating group that you think you might be able to approach. If your interpretation jibes with his, you'll know soon enough. If it differs, you'll know even sooner.

Translators

Interpreters are in many ways like the unarmed Red Cross workers caught between the firing lines on the field of battle. And since most Americans are inexperienced in talking through interpreters, chances are your interpreter will find the source of much of his frustration and battle fatigue coming from your trench. Here are some strategies to prevent you killing off your translator before you've won the battle.

• Brief your interpreter in advance about the issues and the terms that will most likely come up in the course of a discussion. This gives the interpreter time to look up words and phrases before the actual meetings begin.

• Avoid using idiomatic expressions and slang terms that are difficult to translate into another language.

• Speak slowly, clearly, avoiding long sentences and double negatives.

• Try to put your thoughts into two-minute segments at most and let the interpreter translate before you go on.

• Give the interpreter time to make notes on what you are saying.

• Don't become impatient with an interpreter if asked to repeat what you said or explain some point. It's better to take the extra time and be sure that it gets translated correctly.

• Remember that even the best translators will have to use a dictionary occasionally. It is not an indication that the interpreter is incompetent.

• Be expressive. Use facial expressions, tone of voice, hand gestures, and shoulders to convey the tone of what you are saying. The Japanese must wait for the translations just as you do and it prepares them for understanding what the translator will say if they can associate the content of your statements with the accompanying facial and body expressions.

• Japanese and English are two very dissimilar languages,

so don't become alarmed if the translator makes a mistake. The job is not as easy as translating into another Indo-European language and mistakes are bound to happen.

• The translator's job is a fatiguing one. Take a break every hour or two. If you continue to use the interpreter during lunch or at an evening entertainment, for him it's still work.

• Sometimes Americans think the interpreter is "cheating" when a Japanese talks for five minutes and the translator summarizes it in five words. Remember some people are verbose and an experienced translator can often sum up lengthy monologues quite accurately in relatively few words without losing any important points.

Deadlines and Deadlocks

Timetables

Herb Cohen, a well-known American author on negotiation, tells the story about his first assignment to Japan when he was met graciously at the airport by the representative of the company that he would be negotiating with. The plush limousine was waiting, the reps were extremely solicitous about his having a pleasant stay in Tokyo, and everything seemed to get off to a good start. One of the Japanese even offered to reserve the limousine for his return trip to the airport so that he would not miss his flight back to the States. Thinking to himself, "How considerate of them," Cohen gave them his return flight ticket so they would know the hour he needed to arrive at the airport. What he didn't realize was that he was also telling them how long his company had allowed him to strike the deal. He revealed his deadline! And true to the precepts for cutthroat negotiating, the Japanese wined, dined, and golfed him up to the very hour he left to catch his plane. "We piled in [to the limousine] and continued hashing out the terms. Just as the limousine's brakes were applied at the terminal, we consumated the deal." On his arrival back home, his superiors described the wretched and botched terms of the negotiation as the "first great Japanese victory since Pearl Harbor."[1]

The lesson is obvious. The perfect way to ambush your opponent's demands in a negotiation is to back him up against the wall of his deadline where he will probably agree to anything to keep the negotiation from failing. No one wants to go home empty-handed. In fact, a great percentage of business deals are closed just under the wire, whether that wire is strung two days from the first meeting or two months. Knowing your opposition's deadline provides you with an advantageous bargaining position.

The Japanese will probe around for your deadline. Don't give it to them. In fact, use the opposite ploy. Pretend you have all the time in the world. Act nonchalant. They will. At the negotiating table the party that feels the constraints of his own deadline, imagining it to be more imminent than the opponent's, will always be at a psychological disadvantage. So keep cool and do not reveal your deadline. If possible, ignore your deadline since most deadlines are the result of negotiation anyway. If so, they are negotiable and can often be renegotiated.

Deadlock!

Deadlocks are not ipso facto signs that the negotiation has failed. But they are developments that must be handled with the utmost care and delicacy, especially when locking horns with the Japanese. The rough-and-tumble wrestling over offers and counteroffers that delights Americans dismays the Japanese. In general, they do not enjoy bold power plays and the naked display of strength. They are much happier when negotiations resemble the polite exchange of gifts or cups of tea rather than two sumi wrestlers locked in a rib-cracking embrace. Cherry blossoms floating gently to earth is a more appealing image to them than a half-ton of sumi flesh crashing on the sweaty mat. So when you deadlock, you know you have entered a phase of negotiating that the Japanese find distasteful. They will seek to preserve harmony. They want conciliation.

It is important to keep the channels of communication open during this period. Even though you have stopped meeting officially, much can be done behind the scenes. Informally, the go-between can play a vital role in bringing the two teams back to the table. Also it can help to talk to others you know in the Japanese company. Ask them how things are going. Ask for advice. But don't give up hope no matter how long the crisis lasts. When negotiating with the Japanese, a deadlock can last for weeks at a time.

Getting the Seal of Approval

One of the reasons for this is the cumbersome decision-making process they will have to go through with other members and departments in their company before they can present you with a new offer. If you are in Japan, what might be holding them up is the ritual decision-making process, described earlier, called *ringi*. By the time the *ringisho*—the written document itself—has made the rounds, it has the appearance of a group decision with all parties concurring. If the point over which your bargaining deadlocked necessitated a group decision, it could take considerable time.

The compromise that will eventually be worked out will most likely be achieved through go-betweens and intermediaries or some other conciliators that the Japanese engage for the purpose. They will not want to meet you face to face, which to them would create an embarrassing display of power politics. So to save face, their own and yours, they will act through third parties outside the formal sessions. When the final compromise is finished and both teams return to the table, it will appear that neither side was forced into making unwanted concessions to the other. Harmony preserved! Politeness triumphs!

How to Be Graciously Ruthless

In the event of a deadlock, the cardinal rule is to always maintain the *appearance* of harmony, even through the dark nights of the negotiations when it is all too obvious that there is no harmony. Consider this example. When the Japanese realize that they have to make changes in their original position, you may get the impression from the way they explain their new position that you haven't beaten them at all—that it was all their doing! With elaborate and high-flown explanations they will make it seem that the reason they changed (i.e., gave in or gave up) was to move the negotiations to a conclusion for *your* sake. They may talk about their "enormous sacrifices," their "selfless dedication to compromise," or their "heroic offer to promote good will" between the two parties. A lot of sugar-coated *tatemae* to sweeten the *honne* of getting whipped!

The Absolutely No-Fooling Final Ultimatum

Michael Blaker's study of the Japanese international negotiating style warns that the next step after the concession will also be inflated with *tatemae*.[2] The new Japanese position will be described as "magnanimous," "just and fair," "the absolute minimum" beyond which they cannot go. In fact, you may hear them announce their "final" offer several times on several different occasions. And each will be as magnanimous as the last final offer!

This whole question of ultimatums should not rile you. Be prepared to bluff by prefacing your own remarks with comments like "This is the absolute minimum we can accept" or "The way we read the data, this must be our final offer," etc. The Japanese are quite willing to deal with ultimatum lingo as long as you offer escape hatches. Most ultimatums, in fact, leave open several alternatives and are not the black-and-white alternatives most people think they are. While accepting the Japanese "final offers" as "good-faith" proposals, don't be lulled into thinking that they are in fact born of good will. Feel free to refer to their proposals as "highly inflated" or "impossible to reconcile with our needs." The Japanese are aware that the "good faith" being bandied back and forth is as much an appearance as a reality. They know that your company's real needs go beyond good-faith tokens. Nevertheless, the discussion of substantive issues must be conducted within the framework of "good faith and good will."

When you make concessions, do not suggest counter-concessions to the Japanese. Leave it to them to come up with significant opposing concessions. That's their job, not yours. In America, of course, there's nothing wrong with saying, "Look, we'll give you this if you'll give in on such-and-such." But the Japanese want to come up with their own proposals. At least at the conference table they do. You might quietly suggest through a mediator or your go-between what you expect in return. But let the Japanese appear to have come up with your idea themselves when they present it to you face to face.

Closing the Deal

A successful negotiation should leave both parties feeling they have achieved something of value for their time and effort. When the partnership is agreed upon, your side will be ready to write the final contract. The Japanese, however, will not. For them a "heads of agreement" statement is sufficient. Because of the trust and good will with which so much business is conducted in Japan, a finely honed legal document drawn up by lawyers is in their view really unnecessary. They would much prefer an "agreement" consisting of the declaration of intention of both parties. It need not be a lengthy, extremely detailed legal document. So do not present them with a contract. Your lawyers can do the dirty work later.

When the final agreement is concluded, the Japanese may ask you for additional data, information, studies, charts, graphs, etc., just at the point that you presumed it could all be packed safely away. Don't panic and think you've got to make your presentation all over again! The Japanese always want as much information as possible to justify their final position both to themselves and to others back at the company. The hard evidence they ask for will make it easier for them to live with their agreement and with others back home who may be critical of it.

The Contract and Beyond

Because of their experience with Americans, the Japanese know that a contract will eventually be necessary. Out of deference to the Western mania for unquestionable precision —especially in writing—the Japanese will acquiesce in signing a contract. But they don't really consider the contract to be more binding than the spoken word. If you come to an agreement with a reputable Japanese firm on the particulars of a business deal, their later performance will be based on their understanding of the agreement, not on what a contract says nor on any fear of the penalty clauses contained within it.

After the agreement is firmly in hand, resist the temptation to consider the contract sacred scripture. Certainly the Japanese won't. If unforeseen circumstances change the picture so that part of the agreement becomes invalid or impossible to execute, the Japanese will bring it to your attention and suggest the need to renegotiate "in good faith." As Akio Morita put it, the Japanese promise each other that when disagreements arise, they will sit down and talk.[3] Actually, most Japanese contracts have a clause to that effect near the end of the document. And they take it seriously. Even though the American response would be quick to suggest that "good faith" has dissolved if the terms of the contract are not met, the Japanese tactfully and politely return to the conference table. When they make the request for further discussions, don't confront them with "You've got to do it! It's in the contract!" Head for the table.

If there are serious problems with the Japanese fulfilling their end of the bargain, however, a friendly, though firm, reminder or query sent either directly to them or through a go-between will help maintain an ongoing relationship. The key word is tact.

Conclusion

Heraclitus said you can never step into the same river twice. Negotiating with the Japanese is a lot like that. Even grizzled veterans of Japanese-American business arrangements find stepping into business negotiations with the Japanese fraught with surprises, unexpected turns of events, for which years of experience and know-how have not prepared them. You may find the same elusive quality in your dealings with the Japanese. Just when you think you've covered all the issues, achieved a final agreement, and have the contracts drawn up in black and white, the Japanese will undoubtedly discover shades of gray you never noticed. You may not even recognize parts of the agreement when interpreted for you by the Japanese. A twenty-five-year veteran of Japanese horse-trading confessed, "My only job is to handle negotiations for American companies who are involved with Japanese firms and I can't honestly remember a single contract that precisely reflected my understanding of the final agreement. There's always *some* difference between the way I remember our agreement and the way the Japanese remember it." He claims that in spite of the frustrations involved in negotiating with the Japanese, it is in the long run worth it. But watch out, he warns: "It can drive you crazy!"

CHAPTER 6

Going to Work for a Japanese Company: The Perils and the Pleasures

WHEN ASKED WHY he hated craft unions, Sony president Akio Morita's answer was, ". . . all the people in one company should think the same way." The Grand Old Man asserted honestly that the "basic concept of a craft union does not make sense to me." He explained that if companies are going to compete against each other, there has to be a basic agreement and singleness of purpose among employees and management, a harmony that cannot be disrupted by a clash of interests between unions and management. "A job is a job,", he says, and when someone is hired by a company he or she should be willing to do the job on the company's terms. In turn the company will provide for the financial and social needs of its people.[1]

A job is a job. Everyone should think the same way.

Sound stiff? In some ways it is, and yet, according to a 1978 Japan Society report, there are some 81,000 Americans who have so to speak crossed the border and gone to work for or become associated with Japanese companies in the U.S.[2] And there is an additional large number that have relocated overseas. Trading companies, manufacturing and marketing subsidiaries, finance, publishing, advertising, public relations research, design, and even governmental organizations and trade groups—you name it, and you'll find Westerners employed or associated with them to some degree. They have firsthand experience of what it means to work under some hybrid form of Japanese-American organizational management hierarchy and corporate philosophy, which to some extent reflects Morita's dire warning about thinking for yourself or questioning company policies. Not all Japanese companies in America operate the same way, of course, and the 81,000 Americans have a wide range of experiences to relate.

A Corporate and Cultural Safari

For many Americans, the experience of working for and with the Japanese is truly one of the more unforgettable adventures of their lives. In a 1982 seminar sponsored by the Japan Society on the "perils and pleasures" of cross-cultural employment, Americans who either had worked for or were currently associated with Japanese organizations offer a strong word of warning: know thyself . . . and fast! is especially relevant today for someone about to enter the Japanese company's work force. Without a clear, confident sense of one's goals and objectives and an accurate assessment of one's personality, there is a great risk of encountering disappointment, confusion, and trouble. Many Westerners have professional and personal goals that are simply not compatible with, and even clash with, those of a Japanese company. The crucial point is to have a good sense of your short-range and long-range objectives. Do you aspire to become president of a company? Own your own company? Does your current job offer you all the satisfaction that you need? Or are rapid and frequent promotions important? Will you be satisfied just to make a lot of money, or are you really in love with the corporate "cause" to the extent that money is irrelevant? Do you need a job that allows your more flamboyant side to show through? Do you seek a cross-cultural experience as background to some future career? Are you hoping for a particular type of training?

Not only are clear, honest answers necessary to these and similar questions, but you must also have a sense of time, a schedule for achieving your goals. Is it five, ten, fifteen years? For some people a Japanese company may be exactly what their career calls for, whereas others might find that the "perils" may far outweigh the "pleasures" of working for the

Japanese. In the following pages we will look at some of those perils and pleasures in order that you can assess your own situation and know precisely what you may be in for if you join a Japanese company.

Mixing Oil and Water

Not surprisingly, recent studies show that most Americans who become associated with Japanese companies have had no prior experience in dealing with Japanese people or Japanese companies. With little or no orientation and priming as to what to expect, they discover their first weeks, months, even years with the Japanese firm can be nightmarish. We've already seen that "business as usual" does not have a global meaning, translatable from culture to culture. While certain similarities exist between differing national companies (such as objectives for doing business), a multitude of basic differences remains. This is especially true between American and Japanese companies. Some of these differences we have already assessed, such as the different dynamics of decision-making, the incompatible bases of Eastern and Western logic systems, the importance of long- and short-range goals to a company's fiscal policies, and the personal and professional goals of individual employees. Even though a newcomer's intentions are good and his or her expectations are high, and even with a modicum of experience in doing business with a Japanese company, the getting started—not to mention the going!—can be rough.

Diary of an American Advertising Executive

Meet Richard Cartwright. Originally employed by a major New York advertising company to handle accounts with several Japanese clients, Cartwright was later hired as advertising manager for a subsidiary of a prestigious Japanese consumer electronics company headquartered in New York. His story is typical.

"At first it seemed as if I had stepped into the Twilight Zone. I would walk through the company's front doors each morning, and even though I knew I was still in New York City, I might just as well have been transported to a foreign country. I was functionally illiterate in my own country, in my own city! I knew my job would be challenging before I accepted it because I would be representing a Japanese company whose products were sweeping the American market at a time when many Americans were blaming just this kind of foreign intrusion for our own economic problems. But after a few weeks, I realized my problem was bigger than that. I basically had no idea how to work effectively with my Japanese colleagues. Even though my own experience has been in large companies, the Japanese bureaucracy and way of operating was stupefying. My initial impression was that this company, which is one of the most progressive and Americanized Japanese companies in the States, was ineptly run and, it seemed to me at the time, so disorganized that I wondered if their walloping success in the American market was due to luck or some Japanese gods I never heard of!

"I thought my previous exposure to Japanese companies at my former agency would have prepared me, but I was wrong. At meetings I had the distinct sensation that the Japanese considered me some creature from outer space. I was forceful, vocal, assertive, ambitious. I used all the persuasion techniques that had worked in other situations. Nothing seemed to work. To better prepare myself, I started to take classes in Japanese language where I could get to know some Americans in similar situations to mine. At the office I went out of my way to be nice, helpful, considerate to the Japanese. I even ended up compromising my own personality to fit in. But, again, nothing worked. Invariably, I felt like a professional and social outcast.

"I probably wouldn't have lasted very long were it not for my getting to know several Americans who had worked there longer than I. Unlike the others, they were bilingual, bicultural, and had already won the respect of the Japanese hierarchy. They became intracorporate gatekeepers for me, opening doors—and my eyes!—to what was really going on. They clued me in on how Japanese run business meetings, what key political maneuvers were occurring between the Japanese and Americans, and how I could be more generally effective. But the problems continued to exist between the Americans and the Japanese working together, and there just didn't seem enough ways to bridge the gap between the two factors. In fact, you might say that when Japanese and Americans are thrown together in a business setting, a kind of love-hate relationship springs up between them."

The Upstart American

Americans employed by Japanese companies can find themselves caught in a love-hate struggle. Most studies, including the comprehensive ones conducted by JETRO, advise the Japanese to Americanize. They suggest placing Americans in key managerial positions because acceptance of Japanese subsidiaries in America is directly related to their Americanization.

The companies that are attempting to make substantive advances in Americanization tend to be the older companies like Mitsubishi. But in a hundred-year-old company one must expect change to come gradually. There probably won't be major breakthroughs in the ratio of Japanese to American personnel overnight. In the last decade, Mitsubishi's efforts have met considerable resistance by Japanese executives and managers both here in America and in the home office in Japan. Mike Nagai, advertising director at Japan Air Lines in New York, explains that most Japanese subsidiaries here, including JAL, have had a long struggle trying to Americanize management. "It's a very slow process that's been occurring over the last twenty-five years. We're just beginning to promote key Americans to the VP level, but there will probably never be an American president of Japan Air Lines here." At Dentsu Advertising in New York, Mike Pressman, an account supervisor who would most likely be a VP at an equivalent American company, notes that within Dentsu, no American holds a VP title. "Responsibility," he says, "they'll give you. Title is another thing. The Japanese hold on to that."

Yet the Japanese officials are of two minds about the rate and wisdom of Americanization. Not surprisingly, many find it difficult to relinquish companies they have worked hard to establish to Americans with different values and managerial styles. Others do not want to see the plum jobs that have been filled by Japanese nationals (as stepping stones on their way to top positions back home) occupied by Americans whom they feel are less committed to the company and its corporate ideals. Older Japanese veterans frequently prevent rapid Americanization by holding on to their positions of power and maintaining control of the company. Ambitious Americans rising through the ranks are considered a threat to their power; prompted by a sense of solidarity and loyalty to the old system, many Japanese managers find subtle ways to reserve these positions for their Japanese colleagues.

Consequently, there is considerable pressure for an American to prove himself to basically unfriendly colleagues when moved into an important managerial slot. It is also easy to sense the Japanese resentment at having to train Americans who don't speak Japanese, especially for jobs higher than what they were hired at.

Some American personnel officers are uneasy not only with the sluggish promotion policies of Japanese companies but also with hiring practices. In most cases, the Japanese prefer to locate in a region where they will attract a rather homogeneous work force. Their penchant for same-mindedness and group harmony places considerable pressure on personnel officers to hire certain kinds of people, often conflicting with American equal rights practices regarding sex, age, and race. Other personnel problems can arise due to the two-track career program that separates Americans from Japanese. At Panasonic, for example, there are actually two personnel offices, one to handle Japanese employees, the other for Americans.

Neither the Best nor the Brightest

Not surprisingly, many of the brightest American employees leave Japanese firms. Or they don't apply for jobs with the Japanese in the first place. A major challenge facing Japanese organizations is attracting the "best and brightest." When they first opened up offices in the U.S. and were still relatively unknown firms, many were lucky to hire even mediocre American personnel, usually in a sales capacity. Over the years, these first recruits have been promoted to more important positions. Some of them are still there and continue to influence the selection of new recruits who aren't always of the highest caliber. Mediocre financial compensation compared to Japanese salaries, the few chances for rapid advancement, the squelching of personal initiative, and the lack of personal recognition are additional factors that disenchant the brightest American graduates. Marvin Runyon, president of Nissan USA (makers of Datsun automobiles), stated that "Nissan will not compete in the U.S. market in the way of wages, but will only compete on the level of technology."[3]

As a result, the American executive staff of a Japanese company can be of only middling ability, especially when compared with the Japanese staff, all of whom were sent from the home office because of their talent and capacity to benefit both themselves and the company by working in America. A manager at Mitsubishi in New York claimed that only five out of eighty-one American managers were as competent as the Japanese managers.[4] Even an American vice-president at Mitsubishi agreed: "Most of the Americans working for Mitsubishi in a managerial spot couldn't work for American firms."[5] Mitsubishi is trying to hire more MBAs, but even they turn out not to be the best in their class. Larry Bruser, public affairs specialist from Mitsui, believes that a major issue is the overall lack of career development programs available to Americans, as contrasted with those for the Japanese, whose whole career is mapped out for them. It becomes galling to Americans to be working alongside Japanese whose commitment to the company is assured because of the benefits and lifetime guarantees they will enjoy when they return to Japan. "Perhaps," says Bruser, "Japanese companies will change this now that they've recognized the problem, and they will institute career development programs for Americans and thus attract high caliber management."

Group-Think

Among the disadvantages Americans find in Japanese firms are the pressures of working in groups where communication, decision-making, and interpersonal relationships can become complicated. Kneale Ashwell, vice-president of Johnson and Johnson, notes that "while group decision-making ensures that everyone is committed to one goal without any lingering rancor, the system has its weaknesses. If there is a tough decision to be taken, they tend to walk away from it by talking and talking. If you don't have a man capable of making a tough decision, then there's a potential weakness. The beauty of the group system," he adds, "is that you can ignore problems and dodge responsibility. Personal initiative can then be stifled. It's fine if a worker subjugates his personal desires to that of the group, which is what most Japanese do. But we don't want him to subjugate his initiative by refusing to go outside the group."[6] Deference must be paid to those in seniority while maintaining harmonious relationships with peers.

Working in small groups requires intense lateral communication. The need to receive and assimilate input from other departments can be fatiguing for Americans, who often prefer to work alone with a minimum of interference from peers and other departments. The lack of team spirit common among many Americans can account for this. But the blame is not wholly to be borne by Americans. Sometimes Japanese management policies can also be responsible for breaking down harmony between groups. While "the group" is primary and its importance should never be underestimated, in some companies the infighting between groups is like guerrilla warfare, a situation compounded by the policy of concentrating Americans in one work group and Japanese in another. For example, at Sony Consumer Products Company, the Japanese may dominate marketing, while Americans command advertising and sales. Phenomenal feuding can result, taking the form of budgetary and strategy battles where each side is convinced the other is trying to undermine its efforts or supersede its authority. The alleged group spirit that makes Japanese companies so competitive and successful can take a real battering, not to mention the spirit of the individuals involved.

Complicating the communication problems within and between the work groups is the fact that much information is conveyed between Japanese by body language, facial expressions, and hand gestures. Americans usually misread these or fail to notice them altogether. The roundabout manner of conveying wishes and information is frustrating to many American businessmen, who esteem candor and forthrightness, and relish being told a colleague's opinion or explicitly what to do.

Inscrutable Pecking Order

Office politics in a Japanese company are, in a word, Byzantine. In a Japanese firm where there is considerable job rotation, group decision-making, ideas emerging from the bottom up, and managers with a nondirective style of managing, it is usually hard to know just who has the power. For all their critical acclaim, Japanese management techniques have some serious internal problems. An American manager at Nomura Securities in New York complains that "as a rule, Japanese managers are less flexible, unable to cope with rapidly changing events on a timely basis, and unwilling to challenge authority even when the authority is plainly wrong. Japanese managers are more capable when it comes to overseeing boring, repetitive processes."

Even the fabled generation of ideas "from the bottom up" does not always happen in practice, due to the Japanese seniority system. Kneale Ashwell explains, "Japanese tend to be production-oriented. So the people who end up in marketing are the young newcomers in their twenties and thirties, while the sales manager will be in his forties or fifties. The marketing people get drowned by the seniority and their ideas never get off the ground."

Not knowing who wields the real power behind the group or where various co-workers reside in the hierarchy of power, Americans often feel like outsiders, not sure where they belong—or what they're supposed to be doing. One manager working in Sony's corporate development department complained that "not only is it near impossible to know where the real power lies in the corporate hierarchy of a Japanese firm, but the frequent rotations the Japanese make among themselves makes it difficult to get anything done. One day you're working with someone from the marketing department, and the next month he's been sent down to run or work at the Miami sales office. It's like musical managers." He adds that you spend far too much time getting to know the replacements—a fact that is "made all the worse when the new replacement is Japanese."

Sexual Discrimination

Not long ago the following ad appeared in Japan:

> WANTED: 8,000 brides for 8,000 grooms. Young women must be willing to work hard in house and fields. Daily cooking. Also husband's bath preparation. Desire for many children imperative. Must be respectful of and obedient to in-laws.

Why this plea for brides? Japanese women are leaving rural areas in greater numbers than ever before to look for work in the cities. Ads calling for secretaries have lured countless girls from the farmlands with promises of well-paying jobs and a more glamorous, independent lifestyle in the metropolis. But although there is economic opportunity for women in the large and growing corporations and women already make up about 50 percent of the work force, the Japanese corporate world is still a male-dominated bastion of privilege and power. Very few females rise into managerial positions where they would work as equals with male managers. In fact, one estimate is that only one woman in ten thousand ever becomes a manager. Mostly, women are hired as secretaries, clerical workers, and specialists in such areas as research and communications, and discover they have to work much harder and be much better than their male counterparts to gain any professional respect.

In terms of salary, women don't make nearly as much as men. In 1955 women earned 44.4 percent of what men earned; in 1970 it crept up to 50.9 percent; and in 1978, Japanese women earned only 56.2 percent of Japanese male total earnings.[7] Even though a 1974 law established the standard that women must be given equal pay for the same work, the law is so paternalistic regarding women workers in other areas that the protection sections of the law actually sabotage the chances for women to make as much money as their male counterparts. Japanese men continue to view women as physically and intellectually inferior to themselves and, consequently, often do not relate well to women on a business level. Women are seldom considered for promotions and frequently are forced into signing contracts that state they will retire at thirty after only four or five years of work.

Even in the U.S., where women have made considerable headway in their struggle for parity in the workplace, the status of women in Japanese subsidiaries in the States is about twenty years behind the times. The story told by a black woman, bilingual in Japanese and English, and with an MBA from Harvard, is enlightening. When asked about her experience in the market research division of a major Japanese consumer electronics company here, she said, "The amount of sexual discrimination that occurs within the confines of a

Japanese company is comparable to that of U.S. companies back in the forties and fifties. But I was one of the lucky ones. The Japanese didn't really know what to do with a black bilingual female from Harvard. I usually got to call the shots."

Most women employed in Japanese firms here aren't so lucky in breaking through the "old boys network" that is still safely ensconced in the bureaucracy. Take Michelle Russell, for example. After seven and a half years experience in various Madison Avenue public relations firms, she was employed as a manager in the public relations department of a New York branch of a large Japanese bank. Hoping to follow the advice of her mentor at the last firm she had worked for, Russell thought she would stay with the Japanese bank only three years at most to ensure maximum long-term career advancement. She never lasted the three years. After a little over a year, she realized she had no place to advance to but out. She claims, "I was never able to be an effective manager and produce results like I was able to on the agency side. None of the Japanese managers—especially the ones in the public relations department—even rendered me enough responsibility and respect to get a job done. I knew I was capable of performing any job given me. But the fact that I was female meant more to the Japanese. To them, I had no place being in a position of responsibility, no matter how talented or capable I was."

The Bank of Japan recently made an unprecedented move by hiring a female graduate from Keio University to be trained as a manager, the first of her kind. What would have passed unnoticed in America received quite a bit of publicity in Japan, not all favorable. But a token bank manager at the Bank of Japan is no solution to the problem when almost 80 percent of Japanese companies refuse outright to accept applications or interview women, even those with college degrees. The assumption is still strong that women should have menial jobs or jobs that add frills to more serious economic activity, such as "escalator girls" who are hired to stand at the top of escalators and smile at customers as they get off.

Sexist policies such as these have run into trouble in America where the old Friendship Treaty of 1953, stating that foreign companies have the right to hire employees of their choice, openly conflicts with the later Civil Rights Act of 1964, whose Title VII prohibits discrimination against women in hiring and promoting. Recently Lisa Avagliano and eleven other women working for Sumitomo Shoji America sued their employer on the grounds that they were being held back in clerical positions while American men and other Japanese workers were being promoted. Arguing that if a company is in America, it ought to play by American rules, the women brought the case to the Supreme Court and won. The Japanese argument that they needed to promote certain people to "preserve harmony" held no water.

But the outlook is still grim. A female bank manager in Japan or a civil rights suit in America still can't erase the mentality that advertises for eight thousand brides. As Donna Levis discovered after working for a Japanese company, a woman must be willing to risk depression and loneliness when she goes to work for a Japanese firm. Being an American woman doesn't ease the tense situation. The Japanese don't know what to make of career-minded American women, let alone Japanese women who have their sights on managerial positions traditionally reserved for the wise old men of the company. The best advice for women is to think twice and have a clear concept of what career opportunities await you when you apply for a job with a Japanese company.

The Brighter Side

But there is a brighter side to working for a Japanese firm. An American working for the Japanese has a lot to gain, both in terms of professional experience and of personality development.

It has become fashionable in recent years to work for an international company, whether it be American or foreign. Confronted by the reality of living in a global village, interlocking national economies have produced a network of markets and industries, creating enormous international corporations that control the destinies of millions of people. To work for the major companies whose enterprises "shake and move" the world is quite prestigious. To have a career with an intercultural focus is enviable, and people who can add that to their résumés enhance their attractiveness for future jobs, especially in the international business sector. Of all the international companies operating in America today, Japanese firms enjoy a reputation of excellence that extends to their employees. A good position in a Japanese company is an experience that will usually serve as an outstanding qualification and background for a related career change.

Spending several years with a Japanese company can have a profound and maturing effect on your outlook on business and on yourself. As Japanophile Harriet Russell insists, "Greater opportunities exist for Westerners if you're willing to accept the challenge. The cultural differences have to be dealt with in an individual manner, and you should first have a good sense of what the basic differences are." If you don't have this sense when you begin, you will when you leave. The primary opportunities for growth come in the areas of attitude change, especially regarding our sense of time and accomplishment and our understanding of individualism.

Jon Strom, marketing manager for audio products at Sony Corporation, says that working for a Japanese company made him "more humble, less individualistic, and more group oriented. You lose the 'America is the center of the world' attitude," he says. He also discovered that he became a better listener, less aggressive, and more honest about his positive and negative characteristics. At Mitsui, a senior manager said that over the years he found ways to transform his "gun totin' John Wayne style of management" and to defer to his boss, letting him take the honor for major decisions. "I still know how to call the shots," he avers, "but now I do it from behind the scenes."

As Ray Gates, president of Panasonic, claims, "You learn to become more patient. You begin to learn that what you expect to be accomplished overnight in an American company may take days, sometimes weeks in a Japanese company." Others confirm his observation: working for a

Japanese company makes you more able to tolerate ambiguity, vagueness, and indecision.

Another career opportunity that can result from working for a Japanese company is the chance of becoming a generalist by being exposed to a number of different and important aspects of the business which in a similar American company you would never have any contact with. Your professional experience with the Japanese is richer and more challenging. Some Westerners, fortunate enough to be among the first taken in the job rotation training system, find the experience very positive. "Since I've been with Sony," says one regional sales manager, "I've been in marketing, research, advertising, and now sales. I feel as if I have a much more holistic sense of how a business runs as a result." You will learn things that you can take with you later on as you change jobs or even switch careers.

Very few people who work for the Japanese come out the same. Americans with an open attitude about what they will be asked to do can use the experience to develop aspects of their personality. The meeting of East and West can create a richer and fuller personality. You will have to become more group-oriented and overcome some of the individualism that the Japanese find so objectionable in our character. Americans find they have to temper some of the aggressiveness that is ingrained in us from childhood in order to get along well with Japanese colleagues. They learn how to be less selfish when working with others as they are forced to guard against the many sloppy work habits and gruff, self-centered responses that the Japanese interpret as laziness and uncooperativeness. In short, if you work for a Japanese company for a number of years, you should emerge as a more flexible human being, capable of taking a broad-minded approach to new situations, and experienced in getting along with people markedly different from yourself.

Best Bets

From the over 250 Americans and Japanese interviewed for this book, certain options emerge as being the "best bets" for Westerners looking to work for or with a Japanese company. From their own experiences, both positive and negative, here are the general career categories you might consider, with specific recommendations regarding positions and job objectives.

Type of Business	*Comments*
TRADING COMPANIES	Look for large to medium in size, and for management or finance positions. Japanese trading companies are very desirable and a good preparation for newly emerging American trading companies.
HIGH-TECH MANUFACTURING SUBSIDIARIES	This group includes Sony, Canon, Matsushita, and others moving into the fast-growth computer and other high-technology industries. Best jobs and opportunities are in marketing, research, engineering, corporate development, communications.
SERVICE AGENCIES	Seek out American advertising, public relations, market research, and management consulting companies that have Japanese clients. Exposure to the right Japanese clients is potentially valuable later on in your career. Japanese companies will continue to use services of these types of companies in increasing numbers.

FINANCE/INVESTMENT
FIRMS

As Japanese businesses become more international, the Japanese presence in Western financial circles enlarges —e.g., Wall Street, banking institutions, venture capital. Japanese finance and investment "specialists" have already graced American firms with their expertise. A greater number of opportunities, too, will occur for Westerners in the coming years.

LAW/ACADEMIA

Surprisingly enough, while Japanese companies in Japan have inherent disdain for things legal, specialization in Japanese law is on the rise in this country as the growing number of Japanese subsidiaries here require a greater number of skilled practitioners. Also, a number of universities and colleges have MBA, management, and legal studies programs with specialties in Japanese. These will undoubtedly become more prestigious as Japanese business techniques become a mainstay in the curricula.

CHAPTER 7

A Primer for Doing Business in Japan

GETTING INTO THE Japanese market and surviving there can be like an episode out of a James Bond thriller or a Robert Ludlum plot of spy and counterspy, never knowing for certain who are one's friends and who are the enemy. For example, the Japan Tobacco and Salt Corporation is a government-owned monopoly exercising exclusive control over the distribution of all tobacco products, both domestic and imported, throughout Japan. When an official JTS memo, not intended for public consumption, found its way into the American business community, it confirmed the fears of many American tobacco exporters that their products were not being given equal, or even fair, treatment in distribution, promotion, and sales in comparison with Japanese tobacco products. "Curb stocking of imported cigarettes in vending machines," the document exhorted, encouraging suppliers not to stock foreign cigarettes in vending machines that had fewer than ten columns of cigarettes. "Remove displayed items for imported cigarettes in prominent locations," it advised. Japanese retailers responded by tearing down posters and display materials in stores where foreign cigarettes are sold.

When questioned about the disappearance of American cigarettes in vending machines, the JTS complained that they just didn't have enough American brands in stock. Then R. J. Reynolds' "lighted boxes" announcing the brand logo began to disappear from the tops of vending machines. When investigated, no retailers squealed on the JTS. The disappearance of the boxes was blamed on other causes, including, in one case, a typhoon! A proprietress of a small sundries store, when asked if the JTS agents were responsible for her having taken down foreign posters, said only that she wished not to be asked that question.

Despite much U.S. protest to a joint Japanese-American group studying this matter, there is little chance that retailers, who depend on the JTS for licenses to do business, can effectively counteract these moves.

First, the Bad News . . .

Japan is number one in more ways than one. A study commission of seven hundred corporation executives, economists, and labor leaders from twenty-two industrial nations rated Japan the toughest market to crack. Following Japan as the most competitive market to break into was Switzerland, then the U.S. in third place, and West Germany in fourth. Japan's reputation as a nation that does not go out of its way to attract industry from outside its national domain is certainly well deserved. In spite of the recent relaxation of some trade barriers, the almost impervious barricade around the Japanese islands is still there. The soaring trade deficits between Japan and its Western customers are proof. The U.S. deficit topped $18 billion in 1982 and the Common Market's rose to more than $10 billion. Besides limiting the importation of manufactured goods, Japan has aggravated world economic tensions by keeping out agricultural products to appease Japanese farmers. Its shipments of manufactured goods to the rest of the world produces an annual surplus of $100 billion. It's no wonder there is rising resentment of Japan's monetary and trade policies. Even though Prime Minister Nakasone's good will missions have attempted to ease the tension, there is still a strong and growing sentiment around the world for protectionist measures to retaliate against the Japanese.

. . . And the Not So Bad News

Wherever one looks there appears another article either blasting the Japanese closed-door policy or praising Japanese moves to open that door. In spite of the charges and countercharges, American investors still managed to sink money into twenty-two new Japanese projects in 1981, providing more capital for Japanese business than for either French or British firms. A progress report in the *Journal of Japanese Trade and Industry* (November 1982) emphasizes other accomplishments in opening doors to American trade that occurred in 1982. Among these are the improvement of import-screening measures; a lowering of tariff duties in agricultural, mining, and manufacturing products; the relaxation of import controls allowing more herring, pork, molasses, and canned pineapples into Japan; the expansion of the number of retail stores allowed to sell certain items such as tobacco products; efforts to educate Americans about the Japanese distribution system and other business practices by setting up consultant and information services around the U.S.; the liberalization of banking services to assure foreign customers the same treatment as their Japanese counterparts; cooperation between Japan and America in high-technology industries and research programs; and lastly, increased industrial and economic cooperation between Japan and other industrialized nations such as Britain, France, and Belgium.

Yet in spite of these measures, the West is still skeptical, some critics calling the Japanese trade liberalization a "mixed bag" and not the "dramatic" turnabout they had hoped for. In spite of the reduction of tariff and nontariff barriers on some 215 manufactured and farming products, Prime Minister Nakasone admitted in 1983 that the introduction of beef and citrus products into Japan would be difficult due to the strong lobbying efforts of Japanese farmers. Yet the Nakasone government is moving toward the creation of a cabinet-level office to simplify the red tape involved in testing and certifying foreign imports, an agency that would study and make recommendations on over thirty laws regulating standards. But here, too, some Americans think the study commission could be a delaying tactic. Even should a review of standards result in new, more liberalized laws, they point out, lower-level inspectors have been known in the past to ignore them.

Looking beyond all the protectionist hoopla on both sides of the Pacific, there have been some concrete steps taken by nongovernment organizations to facilitate American entry into the Japanese marketplace.

Action Desks

JETRO (Japanese External Trade Organization) placed an ad in the *New York Times* in February 1982 in response to— and retaliation against!—the negative press coverage that Japan was receiving that winter on its refusal to ease barriers to foreign business. The expensive full-page ad, which also appeared in the *Wall Street Journal*, announced that "Japan's Market Is Open for Business" and listed four ways to expand U.S. exports in Japan. Among them were the use of tariff cuts, the reduction of nontariff barriers, and an Office of Trade Ombudsman in Tokyo to speed up action on grievances. Most significant was the offer by JETRO to serve businesses interested in making the plunge. Listing the phone numbers and addresses of five "Action Desks" around the country, JETRO tendered its services to businesses and firms eager to crack the Japanese market. According to the director of the New York JETRO Action Desk, over a thousand responses across the nation had been phoned in. It seemed that American business people were taking seriously Japan's offer to lower barriers to business activity between the two nations. In a similar vein, JETRO also published a booklet listing five thousand products wanted by Japanese companies from foreign countries. Titled "Export Opportunities to Japan," the 130-page book listed the items that over five hundred Japanese firms, both large and small, would like to import from foreign sources.

Business Seminars

Other JETRO activity included the joint venture with the U.S. Department of Commerce to sponsor "How to Do Business in Japan" seminars in twenty-two cities around the nation. Roughly a hundred participants showed up at each seminar location and heard presentations from JETRO itself, Japanese trading companies, various banking institutions, Japanese firms, and Americans who have had success in establishing beachheads in Japan.

American State Fairs in Tokyo

MIPRO (Manufactured Imports Promotion Organization), another commerce-promoting organization similar to JETRO, has held U.S. State Fairs in Tokyo to introduce American products to Japanese consumers. The ten-day fair held in March 1982 attracted 68,255 in attendance. In addition to the fair and other special events, MIPRO gathers information and catalogs from foreign producers and companies which it then shares with MIPRO parties in Japan.

U.S. Trade Missions to Japan

Export development missions sponsored by the U.S. Department of Commerce offer help in entering the Japanese market. Organized around various specialized groupings, such as scientific equipment, food processing and packaging equipment, general industrial equipment, and modern management equipment, the missions include members from a wide spectrum of businesses and geographic regions in the U.S. A large majority of the companies represented had annual sales of under $50 million and two-thirds had never done business in Japan before. The combined group made over three thousand business appointments while in Japan, and on subsequent follow-up it turned out that 70 percent of them had achieved their original goal of creating some kind of business relationship with the Japanese.

State Departments of Commerce

Departments of commerce in a number of states from New York to California can be excellent sources of information and advice on how and what to export. New York State, for example, has a branch office in Tokyo whose aim is to lure Japanese businesses and manufacturing subsidiaries to New York as well as to assist New York companies in their quest for market share in Japan. New York State and others are equipped with area, regional, and even "country" specialists who offer advice and, in some cases, contacts for prospective business partners and/or associates.

Should You Try to Enter the Japanese Market?

Deciding whether or not to enter the Japanese market involves a number of questions and considerations that should not be taken lightly.

First, does your company offer products, technology, or services that could find an international market? If you think it does, then consider whether international growth is really vital to your company. Is Japan in particular important to your company's growth? You may come to the conclusion that your money and manpower could be better applied to the domestic market or some foreign market other than Japan.

Assuming that expansion into Japan is within your corporate goals and objectives, is your company ready for such a move? Is your home office management honestly committed to supporting a Japanese venture? Are you prepared to modify your products and traditional marketing strategies to meet the peculiar demands of the Japanese consumer and distribution system? How comprehensive is your management's working knowledge of international business practices in general and those of Japan in particular?

If you decide that your budget can absorb the overseas venture and that the entire operation will not prove to be more trouble than it's worth, especially to the personnel involved, then you can embark on setting up a Japanese operation. This will include mapping out an adequate working arrangement between the home office, the Japanese office, and any Japanese firms with which you must establish a working relationship. Such a move will be time-consuming, necessitating an ongoing program of market research, adaptation of products, and continuously evolving operational and marketing strategies.

Assuming that your marketing studies and financial projections warrant your attempting a Japanese operation, your next step is to decide how to enter this highly competitive and frustratingly closed market.

How to Enter the Japanese Market

Your first move should be to secure an agent to help in the countless details, procedures, regulatory matters, and other problems that often prove a source of tremendous frustration. Finding an agent can be troublesome, but there are several channels you can go through. The U.S. Department of Commerce and the U.S. Foreign Office offer an Agency-Distributor Service that will come in handy. You can also shop around directly by participating in trade exhibitions such as the ones JETRO has sponsored in Tokyo and in major cities of the U.S., or join one of the U.S. Department of Commerce trade missions to Japan where you can usually arrange interviews and appointments with prospective agents.

SAMPLE FLOW CHART—THE DECISION TO ENTER THE JAPAN MARKET

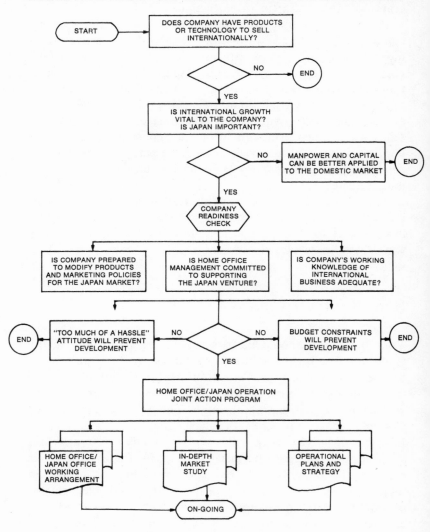

Source: JETRO "Keys to Success in Japan's
Industrial Goods Market," 1981

A Smorgasbord of Agents

There is a tremendous variety of agents available. Japanese trading companies provide many types of services. Depending on whether it is a large, medium, or small trading company, it may deal in thousands of different commodities or specialize in one line of products. There is also the possibility of a non-Japanese trading company or an in-house trade and distributing department in your own company. Sometimes a Japanese manufacturer producing a line complementary to yours can become an agent and distributor. Take Anheuser-Busch's Budweiser beer, for example. It was first imported by the Toyo Menka trading house in 1978. Toyo Menka did manage to sell a modest but still impressive 420,000 twenty-four-can cases that year. However, Budweiser's ultimate success came when Suntory, Japan's largest and most powerful whisky distiller, acquired the importing rights the following year. Suntory's iron grip on distribution made Budweiser the best-selling foreign beer, surpassing even Heineken, despite a stiff price of $1.28 per can versus 78 cents for domestic brews. Suntory expects to sell 1.5 million cases in 1983 alone, up from 500,000 in 1981.[1] If the market for your product is concentrated geographically, you might deal directly with the retail outlet; if the market is scattered across Japan and your product must be sold in numerous small retail stores, you may need an established Japanese trading house that can master the exceedingly complicated distribution system.

In selecting a trading company, you should identify your precise needs and then determine if the company you are considering can satisfy them. Do you need a partner, an agent, a distributor? Can the company provide these services? Know exactly what services and functions you want your trading company or partner to perform.

It is important for you to know the trading company *and the group* to which it belongs. Every Japanese company is associated with other companies, industries, banks, and business associations. Find out who these are, what reputations they have, what they specialize in, how they operate. It is also a good idea to know the financial situation of the trading company you choose. Is it strong or weak? How has it fared through recent business cycles and fluctuations in the world economy? What is the company's philosophy and primary interest? Is it interested in profits, market share, growth, developing new outlets? What has been its prior experience? Learn as much as you can about the experience of the staff with whom you will be directly dealing. Are they accustomed to working with foreign, and especially American, business partners? Are they well-seasoned operatives? What are their backgrounds?

It is important to have an agent you can trust. He knows the ropes, the language, and the people you will deal with much better than an American. Most of all, the agent will have the contacts, and, as we have seen, Japanese business is predicated on knowing the right people and how to deal with them without violating the formalities of their highly complex social structure.

Things Went Better with Coke

One company that broke into the Japanese market quite early and successfully was Coca-Cola. In 1980 the land of *ramune* and cider began to drink "the real thing." Certainly Coke was not "It" at the start, but it became "It" by the end of 1982, when it bottled up about 40 percent of the soft-drink market. One hundred bottles of Coca-Cola drinks a year are consumed by the average Japanese (of whom there are 115 million!). How did Coke do it?

According to Charles Hochman, president of Coca-Cola in Japan, their first task was to develop Japanese partnerships because they needed bottlers and dealers (as well as consumers). So they established "close relationships with local businessmen"—in Hochman's words, ". . . powerful businessmen, respected and with authority in their local communities and able to talk the same language as we do . . . companies with strong management, well established in the business environment, showing great commitment and a real record of success." Hochman's analysis of why so many companies have failed pivots on this point of compatibility: "incompatibility of partners, whether in size or business objectives, or in terms of social backgrounds or types of education of their people, is probably one of the major causes for failure of U.S.-Japan joint ventures." Accounting for Coca-Cola's own success, he maintains that the partnerships created were "truly Japanese in the methods of operation."[2]

The *Journal of Japanese Trade and Industry*, the semi-official organ of the Ministry of International Trade and Industry, makes the same point about partner compatibility.[3] Successful joint ventures are characterized by both partners making substantial contributions because they have a common interest in the business venture. Especially important is the compatibility of the personnel directly involved in the day-to-day operations. And finally, a point that is hard for many Americans to understand fully, is the need to recognize and accept the fact that successful businesses in Japan have got to follow local business methods and practices. Americans must learn to value traditional Japanese ways and accommodate themselves to them.

Some Win, Some Lose

A number of Japanese-American partnerships have failed. Hitachi-Singer was founded in 1973 to sell small office computers. Three years later the partnership was mutually dissolved over the question of whether to expand the agreement to include other Singer products in addition to computers. Hitachi wanted to, Singer did not. Mitsubishi-TRW broke up over Mitsubishi's desire to form another joint venture with Philco-Ford, one of TRW's major competitors. Sterling Drug Company sold its share in Nigata Engineering Company because the pollution-treatment plants and equipment which the two firms had agreed to produce never reaped the profits they had hoped for. When it was dissolved in 1976, the losses amounted to $2 million.

It is especially easy for joint ventures to fold in financially tight times if there is failure to see eye to eye on major policy decisions. A thorny issue over which many Americans and Japanese never come to agreement is the old profits-versus-growth dilemma. In general, the Japanese company will opt for growth and allow profits to sit on the back burner in bad times, while American companies render decisions based on continued profits. Other salient points of conflict frequently discerned in failed joint ventures are selling methods, cost control, strategy, and the use of contracts.

Japan's Free Market Structure

The Japanese market may appear to be a protected environment, but in many respects it is a Darwinian jungle. The fit survive, the unfit die off. Among the proud survivors are Johnson and Johnson, one of the leading manufacturers and suppliers of health-care products; Nestlé, with 75 percent of the instant coffee market in the land of tea drinkers; Lipton, whose name has come to mean "black tea"; Estée Lauder, which, in addition to its line of women's cosmetics, cornered 45–50 percent of the men's cosmetics market; Olivetti, with 40 percent of the portable typewriter sales; Tampax, a leading brand with 30 percent of the market share; Prince, with a formidable share of Japan's tennis equipment market; and Whirlpool, whose appliances are imported through Sony. Just recently IBM-Japan, which is already the second largest computer company in Japan, trailing slightly behind Fujitsu Ltd., announced that it would market a Japanese-language computer (made for it by Matsushita) in order to capture even more of the small-computer market from Japanese competitors on their own turf.[4]

Competition: A Reality without a Name

In spite of the rumors and myths about the "Japan Inc. conglomerate," Japan is a competitive market for foreign concerns. Interestingly, however, the Japanese have no traditional word for "competition." With all its traditions and feudal arrangements that linger into the present, Japan is a cooperative society without a word for a concept that we like to think is a major dynamic in American society. The word *kyoso* has been coined for the concept, but in general parlance it is usually paired with the adjective *kato* to construct the phrase "excessive competition." In Japanese eyes, what we consider normal competition is excessive, out of the ordinary.[5] But it does exist. American companies licking their wounds from their failed business forays into the Japanese market can attest to *kato kyoso*.

Advice from those who have succeeded in the competitive world of Japanese business is never to pull out if you hope to get back in. An American firm must commit itself to weather the financial storms (even typhoons that blow away advertising displays!) for a long time before they hope to show a profit. Loy S. Weston, chairman of Kentucky Fried Chicken, a company that showed a profit after only three years, a rare phenomenon, says, "Unless you have enough money to hang in there for a while, you had better not come to Japan. As a rule of thumb, you should look for losses for the first five to ten years."[6] Jeremy Darby, president and chairman of the Caldbeck Corporation, echoes the same warning: "Japan is not a place where you are going to make money overnight. . . . You have to be willing and able to see no return on your investment for at least five years, and maybe even ten years." His advice is to do extensive market research first and if you have doubts, don't get in. "This is better than coming in and finding out that you have made a mistake and then pulling out. Once you have pulled out, you will never get back in again—ever."[7]

The Home Office Syndrome

Too many companies that fail suffer from the home office syndrome, a complex of attitudes and prejudices that there is only one way to do things: namely, the way it's always been done in Peoria or Baton Rouge. Americans in Japan must be willing to deviate from the accepted norms and venture out to accommodate the Japanese system from importer to consumer. Particularly important is product specialization and concentration. Japanese specifications differ from those in the U.S., and marketing strategies need to concentrate on particular consumer groups. A scatter-shot approach often leaves companies stuck with products that don't fit, taste, or work right for an Oriental society. Another area requiring home office understanding is the matter of delivery schedules, which are tighter and more inflexible than in America. And as in all free market economies, there must be rigorous innovation in design, marketing, and promotional strategies, along with the continuous investment of time and manpower to achieve these innovations. Most of all, the home office must be willing to forego short-term gains in order to become established. If you're fortunate enough to survive beyond the first five years, you may be well on your way to reaping the financial rewards for which you entered the Japanese market in the first place.

Privacy versus Piracy

The Japanese buyer, of both consumer and industrial goods, is a curious animal. Don't be surprised if he asks many questions that make you suspicious of his real motives. The Japanese like to have as much information as possible about potential partners and new products right from the beginning. At times their curiosity seems insatiable. Some veterans suggest that in order not to fear revealing details about your goods and to be perfectly honest with potential buyers, you should have your product or technology patented in Japan before entering into negotiations. Sometimes just telling a customer that certain data are confidential or classified is sufficient to allay his curiosity. But if you must show blueprints or formulas in order to make a sale or create a partnership, it is best to have the Japanese party sign a secrecy agreement. Nothing is foolproof, of course. There is more copying of consumer goods than industrial goods, but a good agent or liaison can explain how to protect your company and product from being pirated.

Legal Hassles

An American company going to Japan will meet a bewildering array of legal regulations. Professional legal advice is a must, and a good trading company can usually answer most questions and provide legal services without the direct use of a lawyer. Some typical areas requiring sound legal advice include:

• The usual health and safety standards that foreign products have to meet. (Sometimes inspections can take three to six months.)
• Import duties can vary considerably from product to product.
• Restrictions in advertising, such as forbidding the use of superlatives in advertising drugs and other pharmaceuticals. (One cannot claim that aspirin X is "the best" or that a suntan lotion gives "the most protection.")
• Many local regulations which can only be obtained in Japanese.
• Maintenance of extensive records and documentation. (The authorities tend to be very strict regarding documentation proving that foreign companies have met all legal requirements.)

Trademarks

It is not uncommon for a Japanese company or private individual to have registered an American trademark even prior to having used it on an actual product. Unlike American law, where prior use is required for trademark registration, Japanese law has no such provision. McDonald's golden arches were registered by a Japanese food company the day before the McDonald's lawyers filed a trademark registration request. That was in 1971. The case is still dragging on. Until it is decided, however, McDonald's has the right to use the arches. General Electric, Neutrogena, even Coca-Cola have had trademark squabbles, as have many other companies. One of the difficulties with the Japanese law is that different individuals can legally own the same name or mark in over thirty different categories of goods. Often the category is determined by the type of shop in which the product is sold rather than according to the international system of designating goods. So, for example, a company manufacturing cutlery may discover that the trademark to its line of knives is owned by someone who has it registered with swords, because it falls into that category rather than into the same class as forks and spoons! Many Japanese want to capitalize on American logos since so many Japanese consumers have toured the U.S. and are familiar with brands and trademarks. Coca-Cola, for instance, is always running into problems with other companies using the logo to decorate small items like T-shirts and ashtrays.

The Great Barrier

Probably the most impenetrable nontariff barrier in the Japanese market is Americans' inability to master the Japanese language. Learning a language sounds formidable, but then so does waiting ten years for profits. Japan is not an easy marketplace to operate in. But those who have shown a marked degree of success have surmounted that impenetrable barrier: they have learned how to talk and do things Japanese.

Banking Services

Japanese banking institutions offer many services to assist foreign companies. Bank officers make excellent go-betweens, not only at the introductory stages of business deals but even later in the ongoing relationship. In addition to introducing new arrivals to their primary Japanese counterparts, the banker go-between can be useful farther down the long distribution line in providing contacts with wholesalers and retailers.

Japanese banks provide data and conduct research for foreign companies in several major areas. They can supply data on the Japanese market for specific products. They usually have the latest information on new technology and product developments in Japanese companies which you may need to deal with or which will be your primary competitors. Japanese banks know which Japanese companies are interested in doing business with foreign firms and which are in the market for purchasing new foreign technology. Banks also carry out extensive research programs to ascertain credit ratings of various companies. Lastly, banks are invaluable sources of information about legal procedures. They have updated information on recent changes in the laws and regulations that cover many types of business operations and activities.[8]

Another encouraging note is that Japan's Export-Import Bank, which has been primarily an export bank, is now becoming more of an import institution, channeling a larger portion of its yearly budget into import financing. In fiscal 1982 only 9 percent went to support imports, but in the future that low figure will be significantly increased.

It's important to understand how a company's cash flow can be tied up in Japan. To a remarkable degree, many business activities are conducted through promissory notes which can have due dates anywhere from 90 to 210 days. Money can be tied up for considerable stretches of time, during which the value of the yen can fluctuate. Careful adjustments in negotiating prices are necessary to reflect both the waiting period and the uncertainty of the value of money at a later date. Foreign companies need to include this time lag in budgeting and other financial projections.

As a reflection of the important role promissory notes play in Japanese business cycles, consider the fact that wholesalers frequently perform financial services within the distribution system, such as lending money to small manufacturers who cannot get bank loans either because their volume is too small or their credit ratings are poor. It is said that wholesalers have more influence in this area than Japanese banks since wholesalers can take a more flexible approach than banks on repayment dates. Money is loaned and deadlines are set by wholesalers via promissory notes that are readily accepted in Japanese business transactions not only by businessmen themselves but even by banks.

The Japanese Consumer

Japan is the second largest consumer market in the free world, following the United States. In the last thirty years the Japanese have become extremely sophisticated consumers as they became more Westernized in tastes and desires. A generation ago, the trend was toward uniformity in clothing and home. Today's modern Japanese are striking out on their own. Part of this shift is due to the rise of the Japanese nuclear family. Clothing and home furnishings are a statement of independence from the extended family of parents and grandparents. Buying patterns reflect the increased leisure time and higher education now enjoyed by the populace at large. More leisure-time products and services are in demand for gardening (tools, fertilizers, plants), sporting activities (equipment, club memberships), travel (luggage, consumer electronics, vacations), home design (furniture, home repair and improvements, hardware tools), handicrafts, and even antiques and art objects. The emphasis is on individuality and self-expression.

In fact, in some market areas and among some consumers there is a decided preference for foreign products, provided the price, design, and quality are on a par with domestic items. In general, the Japanese are so devoted to getting the best buy for their yen that the origin of consumer products is really a secondary concern.

To the Japanese consumer, price is a major indicator of quality. They expect to pay higher prices for better constructed goods. The typical attitude in Japan, as here, is that you get what you pay for. Although they don't feel it is necessary to have the most luxurious or the highest-priced item on the market, they definitely are not suckered into buying inexpensive products that turn out to be cheap in both senses of the word. Not surprisingly, they want durable goods that will last.

The Japanese, like the Americans, are extremely image-conscious in terms of status and peer approval. They look for items that are considered by others in their social groupings as "in" or "best buys." Brand-name loyalty plays a major role in determining future purchases and in advising friends on what or what not to buy. Dealer loyalty is another important consideration, especially in determining the outlets that will carry your products. Quality, price, brand names, and favorite retail outlets all contribute to consumer opinions about foreign products. And those opinions, spread and strengthened by word of mouth, are crucial in determining sales volume.

The Japanese Housewife Calls the Shots

The major decisions about buying and spending on the domestic level are made by the Japanese housewife. Traditionally her role has been that of the record-keeper who receives her husband's paycheck, budgets for family needs, makes most of the purchases, and is in charge of the family's major expenses. She even routinely allocates her husband's daily pocket money! Women in general are a more influential consumer group than men because they are the key to the large middle-class domestic sphere that accounts for most Japanese consumer spending. Women are demanding better home furnishings and a better quality of at-home clothing as they break from the traditional Japanese past of spartan furnishings and the simple kimono for domestic wear.

Service with a (Japanese) Smile

Loyalty to particular brands and dealers comes from a strong history of impeccable service. The Japanese expect after-sales service, and at no extra cost. A story is told about the Japanese who dropped into a diner for a cup of coffee and was given a piece of toast along with the coffee. When he told the waitress that he hadn't ordered toast, she smiled and explained that it was "service." The concept of service includes the handling of customer complaints, which should always be treated fairly, swiftly, and ungrudgingly. As the president of Max Factor explains it, a 365-day warranty must not run out precisely on the three hundred sixty-fifth day.[9] If a customer comes in on the three hundred sixty-sixth or three hundred sixty-seventh day, he will expect that the warranty is still good. Never take a hard line on guarantees in a society that assumes an almost unlimited guarantee period and treats the warranty itself simply as a guideline.

Many Japanese worry about American repair service, especially if the item must be sent back to the U.S. for repairs or if they will have to wait for a replacement to arrive from America. It is a good idea to keep a ready supply of replacements and to be able to perform minor repairs in Japan if possible. Sometimes this can be costly, as in the repair of industrial products requiring a highly skilled engineer.

In the long run, service efforts pay off, partly because of the acute sense of obligation the Japanese feel toward friends and associates. When you give the Japanese customer friendly, no-questions-asked service, you set up an obligation that he or she feels bound to repay. Good service will therefore bring old customers back for more business and encourage them to recommend you to their friends. No matter what it costs or how much time is involved, each time you offer after-sales service, you set up an obligation in the customer's mind to repay the service with more business.

Market Research

Market research is "a foreigner's secret weapon in Japan" according to Andrew Watt, general manager of the Japan Market Research Bureau of the J. Walter Thompson advertising company.[10] It is a must, not only for new firms eager to enter the Japanese market, but even for the well-established companies that have been operating there for years. Hiroya Yano, president and general manager of Nippon Black and Decker, warns, "Even though we are already in the market, we must do market research at least once a year. Even if you are a genius, you can only see half of the changes going on in the marketplace."[11] But market research isn't easy, especially for American companies who have yet to set up operations in Japan.

There are many specialized market research firms and independent agencies in Japan that provide research services. Some advertising agencies also offer market research services to their clients. Not every organization, however, has the expertise to perform all the research that your company may need. Some conduct public opinion surveys; others specialize in consumer and retailer surveys. Advertising research, including television audience measurement, might be a requirement some agencies can't meet. Other specialties include product and packaging testing and motivational research. An American company must know what a Japanese research agency specializes in, who their researchers are, and what prior experiences they have had.[12]

Market research is not cheap in Japan. Costs are high due to the inherent problems of conducting interviews and surveys among a people whose language and communication etiquette, as we have seen, encourages them to save face, be circumspect, and say what they think the questioner wants to hear. This peculiar style of courtesy often skews answers and the *honne* and *tatemae* dynamics of question-and-answer sessions creates further ambiguity. The average Japanese housewife is reluctant to speak openly and honestly with strangers, and the Japanese custom of not letting door-to-door solicitors inside the house means that the interview will probably be conducted on the stoop or outside the door, places where the Japanese are more likely to behave and talk in generalities dictated by etiquette. Most interviews will take place in environments which are not ideal for obtaining the clear, exact information needed for market research data. An added cost arises from the Japanese custom of giving a gift to the interviewee when the session is concluded!

Advertising

All the success stories about American companies selling in Japan have a common theme: massive and costly advertising campaigns. Paul C. Debry, president of Corn Products Company, claims, "What we did first was to educate Japanese housewives. We spent 45 percent of our budget for Japanese television commercials and sales promotion." And it paid off. The blitz worked to convince Japanese housewives to switch from the traditional *miso*, a soybean seasoning, to CPC's corn mix soup. Other American companies, too, can attest to the need for widespread advertising, especially on television. An average of $10 billion a year is spent on advertising in Japan. Thirty-seven percent of that total is for TV commercials; newspapers 33 percent; outdoor ads 15 percent; magazines 5 percent; direct mail 5 percent; and radio 5 percent.

Capturing the television audience is a fiercely competitive undertaking since there are five commercial channels in Japan. Budget permitting, the best strategy is to hit all five channels at the same time. A prime viewing time is the early morning hours, so a company that hopes to keep its products before the viewer will need to invest in simultaneous commercials on all five channels during those peak hours.

It is a serious error to assume that an advertising campaign, theme, jingle, slogan, or pitch that works in the U.S. or Western Europe will grab the attention of the Japanese. Keeping in mind the different classes of consumers within Japan, American firms should pitch their themes to the status consciousness of the group they project as providing the most customers for a given product. Peer pressure and image determine many consumer choices and advertising must reflect this.

Television commercials should appeal to the emotional and affective side of human nature, not the logical or scientific. The Japanese distrust experts and consultants, so overloading an advertising theme with advice, statistics, and scientific studies does not generally sway the Japanese. The soft sell is the preferred, and usually it is the only sell. Ads should aim for a gut reaction with repetitive themes or jingles that let viewers know intuitively that a certain product is "right" and will enhance their positions in their communities. Personal testimonials are popular, especially when given by actors accurately representing the particular social or economic class the ad is aimed at. Kojak and James Bond are common sights on the screen.

Another unique feature of Japanese advertising is that due to the importance of dealer loyalty, the "customer is king" theory doesn't always work in Japan. In fact, as David Gribbin, a senior consultant to one of Japan's leading advertising agencies, puts it, ". . . the dealer, rather than customer, is king."[13] Because of this, a percentage of ads should be aimed at promoting dealer loyalty. These ads, called "in channel" promotion, will require additional advertising budget, but considering the role that wholesalers and retailers play in determining the ultimate sales volume, it is hard to avoid this aspect in advertising.

Americans are surprised to find other advertising costs high in Japan. Although photography—of outstanding quality (as one would expect in the Land of the Rising Lens)—is relatively inexpensive, other production items are costly. Typesetting, mechanicals, copywriting, graphic design, and so forth are more expensive than in the U.S. Furthermore, the role of Japanese advertising agencies is less comprehensive than that of American agencies. The primary activity of ad agencies in Japan is buying media time. Not all of them offer the other services needed to produce a complete advertisement. For example, clients often have to contract for the outside services of a graphic design house or illustrator or create the ad in-house.

Merchandising

Breaking into the Japanese market entails a sincere commitment to adapt the foreign product to Japanese society. Because the Japanese are smaller than Americans, this will necessitate changes in the size of clothing and hand-held equipment. Because Japanese homes have less space, home appliances and furniture will have to be built to scale. Japanese color preferences for various items of merchandise are not the same as Americans' are. And packaging for the "most sophisticated packaging nation in the world" should probably be done in Japan. The Japanese have a long tradition of tasteful and ingenious gift-wrapping, and the modern Japanese has come to equate packaging with quality. Even Japanese weather has to be taken into account; for example, pharmaceutical packaging may require thicker or heavier materials to withstand the humidity in Japan. An obvious packaging strategy is to include the brand name and exterior graphics in both Japanese and English. It is a matter of ingenuity and aesthetics, and Americans should heed the fact that the Japanese eye can discriminate between two minimally furnished living rooms as well as between rocks or trees in a rather spare garden.

A wary Japanese customer will often reject an item if the box it comes in is crushed or ripped. Many times the Japanese evaluation of the quality of a product will include (or be completely determined by) the condition of the finish. A slight chip or mar could convince a customer not to buy a particular brand. An article of clothing unevenly dyed, the edges of a bookcase not perfectly squared, a handbag with cheap lining, sediments in the bottom of a wine bottle—the Japanese consumer, like the American one, will consider all these as indications of poor quality.

Pricing

Since there is a strong tendency among Japanese to equate quality with price, foreign companies must price competitively with other products in the same line. A 10 percent markup over the going price for a quality item is about average. What's important is to create the image—or maintain the image if it's already there—that one's product is as well made as a competitor's. Loy Weston of Kentucky Fried Chicken suggests, ". . . if you are making something which the Japanese are already making—and they are probably making it pretty well—then you had better price competitively and have some extra features."[14] Extra features, of course, include the service allurements and after-sales warranties that mean so much to the Japanese consumer.

The question of pricing boils down to the choice that often makes or breaks American firms in the Japanese market: do we strive for profits or volume and growth? Ultimately, an American company should follow the Japanese lead in this and be willing to live with low profits in the short run in order to capture its share of the market and increase it slowly over several years. Patience and a Japanese way of seeing things are necessary. After all, if an American company really wants to do business in Japan, the most important consideration is survival. Americans have to hang in there and be ready to hang in for a long time.

What's in a Name?

Shakespeare may have thought that what we call a rose would smell as sweet by any other name. Perhaps that's true even in Japan, but the rose-by-another-name may not sell as well. For many types of goods, like cosmetics and fashions, the Japanese believe that a name must be as attractive as the wrapping the item comes in. A recent MIPRO study suggests that "cute, tasteful, easily readable, and easily memorizable names" work best. Japanese consumers can lose interest in products with names difficult both to remember and to pronounce. The story is told of a Japanese company turning down the name "Signorilita" (meaning noble or refined in Italian) simply for the reason that the marketing personnel at the company couldn't pronounce it.[15]

Made in Japan?

An important decision is whether to import from America or manufacture in Japan. There are no easy answers. It is extremely costly to manufacture in Japan. Labor and material costs are very high. Moreover, a domestically manufactured product, even when made by an American company, loses a bit of its foreignness, and in some cases being foreign is a promotional advantage. On the other hand, importing runs into the problem of damaged goods and the perennial issue of how much to stock. The struggle to maintain adequate supplies often means steering a perilous course between the risks of overstocking and understocking. Many American firms suggest keeping a two-to-four-month supply of most products. Hiroya Yano says the "supply situation [is] very inflexible" and no matter how good your long-range forecasts are, estimates of future sales are "at best very educated guesses."[16] Many companies find that they simply have to overstock, rather than get caught short, and just pay the additional storage and warehousing costs.

Some companies can take advantage of the merchandising and promotional services offered by major wholesalers with whom they do business. Established companies enjoy a vast network of channels and contacts in the domestic market. Utilizing these connections, wholesalers can survey and analyze market trends and report back to their clients valuable information that will help determine merchandising and promotional strategies. The larger companies that are engaged in international trade even offer advice on overseas ventures as well.

The Distribution System

It's been called the most confusing in the world even by Japanese organizations committed to making it more accessible to the outside world. In some cases the distribution network is the result of generations of personal favors and obligations. Parts of it almost defy logic and what Westerners would consider sound business practice. To the outsider it is an enigma. But the Japanese face it, too, and the outsider must admit that no matter how much everyone complains about it, it works. Most of all, the advice you will hear everywhere is, don't try to buck it. It's the system. As Jeremy Darby of Caldbeck puts it, "One of the lessons that one learns quickly here is 'Don't try to buck the system.' If you try to short-circuit the Japanese system, you generally come unstuck."[17]

How Does It Work?

Basically it works like most other components of Japanese business: through a complex pattern of human relations. Warner-Lambert's Yutaka Saito explains how in some cases the pattern is based on blood lines. "The grandfather of the retailer perhaps knows the grandfather of the wholesaler and the father, etc. They have such a close relationship that the wholesaler just comes and puts merchandise on the retail shelf."[18] Like Japanese society at large, the distribution system is a network of trust, understanding, and mutual obligations among people who share a remarkable single-mindedness and homogeneity.

Room for One More

Statistically it has grown out of proportion to what would be considered a workable distribution system in the West.

However you look at it, it seems unwieldy. There are about 1.4 million retailers in Japan, or about one for every eighty persons. This is about twice as many per person as you will find in America, Great Britain, or France. In addition, the size of the average retail establishment suggests the survival of the old mom-and-pop variety store that has been disappearing in the West. Nearly 90 percent have floor space of less than 200 square feet, and the number that have more than thirty employees is less than 1 percent. About 85 percent of the retailers have less than four employees; these are truly the one-family enterprises.[19]

The wholesaler's situation is equally surprising. Again, there are about twice as many wholesalers per person in Japan as in the U.S., about one for every 323 persons. About 20 percent consist of only one or two employees, roughly 70 percent have nine or fewer employees, and only about 3 percent have over fifty workers. The ratio of wholesalers to retailers in Japan is approximately five to one, while in the U.S. there are only 1.3 wholesalers to every retailer.[20] Clearly, the network of relationships and channels through which goods must flow to reach the customer can appear formidable to the outsider.

The reason there are so many retailers and wholesalers in Japan is that the best shopping areas are near commuting stops on the bus routes and along the railroad. Over the years small independent shopkeepers have opened stores and become entrenched. In general, the smaller the retailer (or the producer, for that matter), the more intermediaries are needed to deliver merchandise. So what has resulted is a long, confusing network of producers, wholesalers, and retailers through which both Japanese firms and foreign companies must compete to get to market.

A Newcomer

Recently an alternative to the small mom-and-pop stores has sprung up, consisting of the supermarket chains typical of the West. The formula on which these chains succeed includes self-service in a centralized shopping center type of environment. Stores usually have limited stocks of goods in order to carry more brands. Although they are not convenient for many Japanese consumers, they manage to undersell the smaller shops and the larger department stores by about 10–20 percent on most items. There are over 10,600 self-service stores in Japan, but their business accounts for only about 10 percent of the total sales. Department stores make up about 14 percent. The remaining 76 percent occurs in the small retail shops. If the self-service stores continue to spread, they may be able to alter the distribution system; already they have eliminated the need for various layers of distribution.[21]

Parts of the Puzzle

What behavioral patterns and financial obligations should you expect to encounter once you plunge into the labyrinthine Japanese distribution system?[22]

First of all, it helps enormously to have a *Japanese partner* or agent to show you the ropes. Since the initial requirement is to make contacts, then establish and cultivate personal relationships with wholesalers, middlemen, and retailers, a Japanese agent can meet the language and etiquette requirements better than you would be able to do on your own. Furthermore, a native will know the various routes and channels through which goods could flow and be able to advise which is best for a given product.

The *rebate system* pervades the distribution network. Although the idea of rebates is nothing foreign to Americans, the Japanese distinctions between the different types of rebates border on the inscrutable. There are over five hundred different types of rebates, determined by purpose, function, etc. There have been attempts to rationalize the system but to no avail. Much rebating involves confidential information between the parties concerned, and between old cronies the established practice is to decide the amount or type of rebate on a case-by-case basis.

Frequent deliveries are the norm in Japan. Since so many of the retailers are small operations, large stocks are out of the question. Consequently, some items like drugs, food, and home appliances require daily shipments to keep shelves stocked. In most industries there is no minimum order, so each customer expects deliveries from his supplier based on individual need, amount of business, or storage space.

Return privileges are exceedingly liberal. Again, because of the small size of most stores, shopkeepers cannot allow unsold stock to remain on the shelves very long. There is an acute need to maintain a steady and reliable turnover. So wholesalers allow a considerable volume of returns of unsold merchandise, rather than limiting returns to damaged goods as is typical in America.

The use of *promissory notes* is perplexing to foreign companies operating in the Japanese distribution system. Since the retailers are small and conservative, they are not great risk-takers when it comes to tying up capital. Their financial resources are limited, to say the least. As a result, the practice has grown up of wholesalers acting as credit agents for many small entrepreneurs. They sell goods to retailers on consignment with liberal return privileges. Needless to say, such a system can tie up considerable amounts of capital for long periods of time.

Pricing is quite competitive. In order to boost sales, there are frequent price wars. Again, the size of the shop and the need to keep merchandise moving account for the special low-price sales. The family-run nature of so many stores also encourages low prices in order to increase volume because overhead is not perceived as a major expense. In fact, some families consider labor cost as zero. Competitive pricing has practical implications for merchandising in terms of offering attractive products that cater to consumer tastes and build up consumer loyalty.

Incentive plans are another major feature of the distribution system. Dealer aids to encourage sales are a must in many areas. In some cases these might take the form of giving the dealer a percentage for selling a certain volume or more. Expensive bonuses even include trips to the U.S. or vacations at Japanese resorts. Less expensive but effective incentives are theater tickets, dinners, managerial information, and display kits and promotional materials.

Company goals must reflect the delaying aspects of the Japanese distribution system by settling for *small returns over long periods of time.* As we have seen elsewhere, the name of the game is patience. Profitability cannot be rushed.

What About Your Own System?

The possibility of establishing your own independent distribution system is a viable option for some companies. Nevertheless, independent networks have many of the same features as the Japanese system, like the need to create personal relationships among a large number of retailers. Making the constant small deliveries can be exceptionally expensive. If your product is sold in a concentrated outlet, however, such as department stores, rather than scattered across the nation in small shops, you can sometimes dispense with numerous middlemen. You might discover, though, that when selling through one department store you alienate others. Scott R. Izat of Dunhill warns that "Once you are going directly to one department store, then no other department store is likely to deal with you because you are dealing with their rival."[23] The solution is an independent distributor who has contacts with more than one department store. Or another option, as in the case of Kentucky Fried Chicken, is to consider opening a line of franchises and then distributing through the franchised dealerships.

However you cut it, the Japanese distribution system is cumbersome and difficult to deal with. But it can be done. Good personal relationships, Japanese contacts, patience, and a willingness to go along with the system, no matter how obscure it may seem from a Western point of view, will increase chances of a profitable success.

Setting Up an Office

One of the first steps in setting up an office and hiring personnel in Japan is to find a reliable adviser. Many legal and procedural hassles are made immeasurably easier by someone whose experience and advice can cut some corners. Usually an older, seasoned veteran of Japanese society, someone over forty and with ten or fifteen years experience of living in Japan will suffice. The adviser does not necessarily have to be a Japanese. An American who has been around, knows the ropes, and has the contacts will do very well. The adviser should be consulted and often be physically present for most negotiating sessions and at many of the stages of settling in: renting space, staffing, housing American staff, deciding on expense accounts, recruiting sales personnel, initial training, and public relations decisions.

Finding Space

When procuring office space, it is necessary to have a license for a sales office since by Japanese law a sales office that produces income is considered a trading company. A simple liaison office, however, which does not produce income does not need to be licensed.

There are a few things to remember about leasing office space. Some leases are considered "termless" and can be ended on six months notice by the landlord or immediately by the tenant. Confusion can arise because many "termless" leases state the number of months or suggest infinity! If your lease is specifically for less than twelve months it is considered termless. Likewise a lease that has some vague clause about "forever" or "indefinite" is termless. A minimum lease in Japan is one year, the maximum twenty years. Foreigners also need guarantors before drawing up any lease.

Hiring Personnel

Hiring Japanese employees presents unique problems for American companies. The lack of mobility in Japanese business life prevents any large pool of experienced workers, especially in middle- and upper-management positions. Headhunting agencies, although there are some, have not proven to be a very successful way of recruiting executives and managers. Most higher-level employees stay with their firms for life. The best way to interest talented Japanese personnel is through personal acquaintances. Often your contacts will know of experienced, older executives soon to retire into less interesting jobs or men who are no longer up for promotions at their companies and are willing to relinquish their benefits for a better job. For less-skilled or lower-level jobs, an advertisement in the newspaper soliciting applications and followed up by interviews works well.

In seeking top-notch Japanese personnel, JETRO's advice is to be a bit suspicious of bright, young, aggressive Japanese managers who are willing to leave their companies to join U.S. firms.[24] One should question why they are giving up lifetime employment and fantastic benefits to work for a foreign company. In Japan, working for foreign firms is not considered as prestigious as working for a Japanese company. Also, in Japan, as in the U.S., the brightest students are recruited right out of college to work for the best companies. And in general, the Japanese prefer to work with other Japanese, so the more Japanized your company is, the easier it will be to recruit more Japanese employees. It may sound like another Catch-22: you can't hire good Japanese workers unless you already have good Japanese workers. Hiring talented Japanese employees is a competitive enterprise in itself. Some veterans conclude that it is easier to attract experienced personnel than to hire younger people and have to train them. Of course, recruiting older, experienced people costs more money. And sometimes offering higher salaries than other companies cannot win over certain Japanese among whom stability is a more important career consideration than salary. So it is a dilemma.

A cardinal rule about evaluating Japanese who apply to work for foreign firms is not to be misled by their ability to speak English. While it is important to hire English-speaking nationals, it is a mistake to think that their ability to speak English is a sign of their brilliance or experience. It only indicates they have an aptitude for learning a foreign language and/or that their experience has included association with English-speaking people.

Women

More and more Japanese women are entering the work force, but usually only on the lower levels of secretarial and semiskilled or skilled manual work. And they tend to stay there. Because Japanese society as a whole is not as advanced as Western societies, women are still considered the workhorses of Japanese business and are given the lower-paying, less prestigious jobs. Only about one woman in ten thousand ever rises to a managerial position.* Generally speaking, women are not considered for promotions to levels where they will work as equals with men. The old geisha tradition is still strong, even in the corporate world: women are there to please and work *for* men, not with them or over them.

Hiring American Staff

Americans holding positions with U.S. subsidiaries in Japan should serve longer periods of time than in similar jobs in other foreign countries. Because Japanese society is so alien to most Americans, it takes a good deal longer to become acclimatized to Japanese customs and thinking. When replacing departing Americans with new arrivals, the overlap time

* See Chapter 6, "Going to Work for a Japanese Company," pp. 125–141.

should be longer in order for the newcomers to ease themselves into the foreign setting.

For the most part, Americans arriving in Japan have not been well trained, briefed, or schooled in what to expect. Reports have shown that almost no company trains its employees to a "working proficiency" before sending them to Japan. They know very little about the customs, rules of etiquette, peculiar ways of doing business, and very very few can speak the language adequately. Recommendations from commissions that study the problems Americans encounter while working in Japan include the need to train the American worker's family as well, so that the family unit can adjust to Japan together. It does not help an American businessman's adjustment if he has to deal with culture-shock problems during the day and then go home to a family that is as confused and unsettled as he is.

American Managers with a Japanese Style

As seen in earlier chapters, the type of American that works out successfully in a Japanese company and makes the best manager is the one who can preserve peace and harmony among his colleagues and fellow workers. Knowing how to keep quiet, enduring others' weaknesses and peculiarities, having a live-and-let-live attitude—all of this helps to establish the harmonious, trusting work relationships that are a must when doing business in Japan. Human warmth is important, although in Japanese parlance, relationships are "wet" (close, obligatory, and highly interconnected) rather than "warm" (just friendly and nice). "Sticky" (necessarily interdependent) is preferable to "dry" or "cold" (merely cordial). So a "wet, sticky" personality will make the best manager in terms of being accepted by his Japanese staff.

The day-to-day running of a Japanese office will present situations and challenges far different from those of the parent company at home. Most American offices in Japan run best when the American presence is subdued and unobtrusive. An obvious way to achieve this is to have instructional manuals and signs translated into Japanese. It comforts the Japanese working for you when the atmosphere is not heavily American. It's necessary, however, to have Americans in key positions for reporting back to the parent company. It's been found that even the most capable Japanese personnel will write reports according to their cultural biases and perceptions. It strengthens accurate communication between the Japanese and American offices to have it done by Americans.

Japanese Managers in American Companies

For long-range stability it is best to have Japanese managers wherever possible. Since they are often committed to their jobs for life, they bring the stronger dedication to their work that is sometimes missing among Americans who are interested only in the success of the few years they will spend in Japan. In other words, the Japanese manager can be more enthusiastic and committed to future goals than the American whose primary goal is simply to leave the Japanese subsidiary in good shape when his tenure ends.

A further attraction in having Japanese nationals as top-level executives and managers is that they know their own culture inside and out and can perform those necessary go-between tasks that are always present. Ideally, if a Japanese manager has worked or studied in the U.S. for several years, he brings an even more valuable skill: being able to interpret the cultures to each other and to function masterfully in both. No matter how long an American works in Japan, there will always be areas in which he is weak. David Phillips, a Japanese in spite of his name and a managing director of Morgan Stanley and Company Tokyo, puts it quite bluntly, "It is particularly difficult to do business in this country without knowing the behind-the-scenes business customs. A lot of it is instinct, a feel. The formal statement someone makes in a business deal in Japan is one thing, but the substance is often another thing altogether." So if a company is lucky, it will find personnel like Phillips who have been trained and are experienced in both cultures and can provide the bridge between the two.

No matter how one fights it, the "home office syndrome" plagues most American companies operating in Japan. Things are done differently there, and the home office must trust the Japanese staff. There are many issues that can and will become potential powderkegs if there is not a smooth line of communication, understanding, and trust between the home office and the Japanese office. Questions relating to decision-making, translations, the need for additional meetings, the dilemma of profitability or morale—these and other issues can easily lead to massive breakdowns in communication. Every effort should be made to keep the lines of communication as open as possible. Even returning personnel, who have sworn to themselves that they will not fall back into the home office syndrome of doubting and questioning the way their counterparts in Japan are running the company, discover that after a given period of readjustment to the American way of doing things, they become just as suspicious and distrustful as those who have never worked on Japanese soil.

Conclusion

When all is said and done, Japan remains a surprising and contradictory society in which the American company will never be quite at home. When compared to American subsidiaries in other nations, those in Japan confront a monolithic culture that, in spite of its attempts to have an open-door policy toward the West, continues to be Oriental to its very core. It is out of that central core that Japanese business culture springs, and unfortunately for Americans working in Japan, it is that core they will never fully understand. But in spite of the subtleties and nuances that Americans find difficult to come to terms with, there is ground for optimism. The door really is opening wider all the time. Even when it was closed tighter than it is today, companies like Ford, Levi

Strauss, Black and Decker, Kentucky Fried Chicken, Coca-Cola, Max Factor, Johnson and Johnson, Olivetti, Canada Dry, Schick, even IBM, and a host of others, became household words in Japan. As opportunities continue to increase for American companies, other brand names—perhaps yours —will become just as familiar.

CHAPTER 8

A Baedeker for Business: A Compendium of Key Concepts and Ideas

WHAT FOLLOWS IS a compendium of key terms and concepts that have been examined in the previous chapters. They are grouped here under three convenient headings: 1) "Personal Behavior and Attitudes"—the traits and facets of both personal and professional relationships between East and West; 2) "The Japanese Company"—the salient features and procedures which contribute to the uniqueness of the Japanese firm; 3) "Doing Business with the Japanese"—the actual process and dynamics of dealing and negotiating with the Japanese, all the skills and wiles you'll need in order to be the business partner the Japanese can't refuse.

Personal Behavior and Attitudes

Amae: This Japanese term signifies the feeling of being nurtured and cared for; a warm, loving relationship that gives one a sense of belonging and acceptance; a condition that characterizes most Japanese relationships, both familial and professional and that they find lacking when living and working in the U.S., thus creating the impression that American society and business relationships are cold and unfeeling.

Apologizing: Apologizing is a social ritual in Japan that colors most conversations; quick to say "I'm sorry," the Japanese find Americans too brusque and insensitive about others' feelings; for the sake of smooth personal relationships with the Japanese, Americans should use statements of apology as a matter of fact and diplomacy.

Criticism: It is not appropriate, according to Japanese custom, to criticize someone openly, thus causing him to lose face; embarrassment should be avoided whenever possible by refraining from negative or combative statements that will make the Japanese look wrong or foolish.

Deference: The Japanese have a strong sense of hierarchy and rank on both social and corporate occasions; formal respect should be paid to persons with titles or in positions of authority, especially in group situations such as meetings.

Hypocrisy: Because Westerners are so unfamiliar with the skillful manipulation of *honne*, the actual substance of an issue, and *tatemae*, the form in which it is presented (or in which one desires to present it), we often interpret actions of the Japanese to be duplicitous and dishonest, and accuse the Japanese of insincerity and deceit. In fact, the use of *honne* and *tatemae* by the Japanese is probably one of the most artful, legitimate, and effective tools in the bargaining and negotiation process. Understanding the dynamics behind the process may be your ticket to success. For the Japanese, *honne* and *tatemae* are more than a negotiating tool. The discrimination between *honne* and *tatemae* arises out of the inexorable need of the Japanese to save face. What Westerners interpret as hypocrisy or deceit is, from the Japanese viewpoint, a pragmatic and culturally necessary tactic for preserving surface harmony.

Inscrutability: The Japanese, like other Orientals, are considered by Westerners to be inscrutable; it's true that there are many things that a neophyte will find unfathomable, but like all people, the Japanese become easier to read as one gets to know them. It is important not to mistake inscrutability for hypocrisy or lack of sincerity; gestures and comments that mean one thing to the Japanese are often interpreted to mean the opposite by Americans, thus perpetuating the stereotype that the Oriental can never be understood or trusted.

Language: Probably the greatest barrier to cross-cultural and professional business dealings with the Japanese is language. Very few Americans are bilingual; the Japanese who speak English find it difficult to understand nuances and American idioms. Americans must therefore be extremely sensitive to the language barrier, speak slowly, avoid obscure terms and phrases, and be willing to repeat statements as often as necessary to achieve understanding.

Logic: Probably the second greatest barrier to cross-cultural business dealings with the Japanese is the difference in logical mode. Although the Japanese will often seem to be thinking or acting in an illogical manner, Westerners must realize that the Japanese do operate according to logic but that it is a different logic from our own. Appealing to reason as we define it is not as forceful an argument in dealing with the Japanese as taking an affective, intuitive, emotional approach.

Nonverbal Communication: All peoples express themselves in nonverbal ways. The nonverbal indicators employed by the Japanese are different from American ones; and nonverbal forms of communication are more often used by them than by Americans, who frequently fail to notice or understand meaningful gestures, facial expressions, changes in breathing patterns, etc.

Politeness: Westerners have a tendency to mistake the politeness of the Japanese for friendship, not realizing that because of cultural conditioning the Japanese tend to be exceedingly polite and considerate to strangers. Never think that their polite "friendliness" is the same as friendship; public demonstrations of intimacy, such as the use of first names, a friendly slap on the back, and other such gestures are considered rude and offensive by the Japanese.

Saving Face: This is a basic form of etiquette practiced by the Japanese both among themselves and with Westerners. It often involves the concepts of *tatemae*, form, and *honne*, substance; in unpleasant social or business situations, the substance of the problem will be conveniently glossed over by the proper form; sometimes the need to save face will result in ambiguous statements or what appear to Westerners as white lies in order to preserve group harmony and self-respect.

Status: Japanese society is extremely status-conscious; while it may seem old-fashioned or anachronistic to Americans, it is important to understand the rules of etiquette and conduct relating to status so as not to violate a social taboo or offend someone by disregarding the courtesy due him.

Superiority Complexes: While both Americans and Japanese have legitimate reasons for imagining they are superior to the other, and each national group can "best" the other at some things, it is important, especially for Americans, to avoid the "America is the center of the world" attitude; many Japanese express a desire that Americans be more humble and boast less about the American way of doing things.

Upward Mobility: Americans expect job mobility with concomitant raises and rapid promotions; many expect to change companies or switch careers sometime in their lives; most Japanese, on the other hand, tend to stay in one or two jobs their whole lives and view American restlessness as a fault they do not readily understand.

The Japanese Company

Americanization: Americanizing Japanese subsidiaries in the U.S. is a thorny dilemma for Japanese company directors. American job-seekers are reluctant to apply at companies that seem "too foreign" in management and work codes, but too much Americanization too quickly can weaken the Japanese methodology and managerial style that accounts for success in quality production; furthermore, many Japanese nationals are reluctant to relinquish lucrative positions in their subsidiaries to Americans, jobs they often use themselves as stepping stones on their way to the top and to eventual return to the home office in Japan.

Corporate Philosophy: Major companies have a clearly defined philosophy, a statement of principles and ideals by which employees are expected to act and think. Concerns addressed include service, quality, loyalty, hard work, and cooperation. Corporate philosophy is expressed in such forms as songs, slogans, placards, posters, and employee recreational activities and entertainments.

Group-Think: Because harmony and agreement are so important in Japanese corporations, employees are expected to suppress personal desires and differences of opinion in order for the group to achieve unanimity on major decisions; Americans working for Japanese often find that this stifles creativity and that the pressure to be supportive of others forces them to compromise personal and cultural values and habits regarding self-expression, forthrightness, and the right to dissent. Often the Japanese do not understand the American view of work as primarily a livelihood or the American preference for quitting at a scheduled hour and spending most evenings and weekends with family and friends.

Japan Inc.: A Western characterization for the tremendous coordination among Japanese businesses, banks, and government, the term errs by suggesting that the country operates as a monopoly, undivided by special interests or competition. While there is much government planning and support, the phenomenon called "Japan Inc." should be considered a "negotiated interdependence" that has evolved rather naturally in a very homogeneous island society where horizontal integration and a complex distribution system have produced a level of understanding and coordination among various segments of the business community unknown in America.

Job Description: Job descriptions are not given in Japanese companies as they are in American ones; this is often frustrating for Americans who work for Japanese firms. New recruits are expected to learn their duties and responsibilities on the job rather than from a written description; the lack of written guidelines often makes many Americans feel inept and clumsy when learning a new job at a Japanese firm.

Job Rotation: Rotation is a process of acquainting Japanese employees with various aspects of the company; a Japanese worker will usually hold several positions in several departments in the course of his work life. According to the Japanese managers, this procedure, besides creating generalists instead of specialists, makes for harmonious, understanding relationships between individual workers and between company departments.

Lifetime Employment: Most Japanese who work for major corporations will stay with their employer for their entire work lives. Fabulous benefits, automatic raises and promotions, and early retirement benefits, not to mention job rotation and company-specific skills, help to stabilize the company work force; commitment to lifetime employment also necessitates retraining for individual employees who are transferred to other divisions and work areas. Rarely will an American subsidiary of a Japanese company offer lifetime employment.

Organizational Development Departments: The ODDs are an essential link between parent companies and their international subsidiaries; agencies set up within the parent company and freed from the necessity of showing a profit, their primary concern being to facilitate corporate needs and communication between the home office and the company representatives overseas. Without ODDs Japanese firms would not have the data, resources, contacts, and political clout in foreign countries which they presently do and which play a tremendous role in their success in infiltrating foreign markets.

Profits: In Japanese companies, top-level managers are likely to forego profits for as long as five to ten years when penetrating a foreign market; unlike American companies, whose short-term goals include the dollar return on investments, Japanese firms are willing to sacrifice short-term profits for long-term market share, a frequent source of disagreement between Japanese and American business partners that causes the demise of many Japanese-American ventures.

Promotions: Like salaries, promotions are automatic and result from years spent with a company rather than from exceptional performance; often promotions do not occur swiftly enough to please Americans working in Japanese companies, and this is one of the frustrations that make many Americans resign.

Quality-Control Circles: In Japan, groups of about fifteen people from various levels of a department or company are assigned to study problems and suggest methods of maintaining product quality or service. This mode of participatory problem-solving encourages and stimulates individual workers to have a more active concern for the success and reputation of their companies. It has been adopted with varying success by some American companies.

Ringisho: This document detailing a group decision is circulated to secure an official stamp of approval from each of the major participants in the decision—often a slow, time-consuming process to achieve unanimity and squelch dissent. The document indicates the intention of the signers to support the agreement as well as to execute its recommendations. This procedure usually is not practiced in American subsidiaries of Japanese companies due to the hybrid (Japanese/American) nature of management.

Salaries: There is not as wide a gap in salaries earned by top executives and lower-level managers in Japanese companies as in American ones; raises are automatic according to seniority, and are not given for outstanding services. Salaries are not always considered rewards or expressions of personal worth as in American companies.

Sexual Discrimination: The goal of equal rights for women is not nearly as advanced in Japan as it is in the West; Japanese men are accustomed to regard women as inferior, both physically and intellectually; consequently women in a Japanese company generally occupy subservient jobs—secretarial, clerical, communications, research. There is not much opportunity for promotion to managerial positions. Career opportunities for American women with Japanese companies to date are understandably limited.

"Slow, Slow, Fast, Fast": The phrase is a characterization of Japanese decision-making and implementation: decisions are made cautiously and slowly but implementation is swift—the reverse of most American practice.

Sogo Shosha: These are the large Japanese trading companies that over the years have become indispensable agents for facilitating the enormous growth of Japanese export trade; operating in other nations as well, the *sogo shosha* have become involved in the international trade of many countries around the globe, offering the services of their far-flung contacts to non-Japanese clients as well.

Work Groups *(Ka)*: Most work in a Japanese company is performed by various work groups which take the rewards and the blame for the final product; great effort is made by the group members to suppress personal desires and preserve group harmony. Cooperation is a key value and each member of the group takes the attitude that whatever is necessary must be done by whoever is able to do it at the time.

Doing Business with the Japanese

Deadlines: The Japanese are notorious for using knowledge of their opponents' deadlines to drag out negotiations to the last minute in the hope of quick final acceptance of their terms. Keep your deadlines confidential or, if possible, flexible so that you will not be backed into a corner and have to make decisions under duress.

Entertainment: The Japanese are hardy entertainers and spend long hours on the town with business associates; while they are somewhat puritanical about work hours, the reverse is true during after-hours entertainment. A significant amount of the corporate budget is allocated for entertaining; in fact, about the only way to really get to know your Japanese counterparts is in the relaxed atmosphere of a restaurant, a cocktail lounge, or at the theater or sporting events.

Go-Between: An important social and professional function in Japan has traditionally been played by the go-between. Today business ventures require him; he arranges introductions and initial meetings and facilitates the settlement of disputes that arise later on. Americans seeking to do business with Japanese both in the U.S. and in Japan should find some respected third party well known to the Japanese company under consideration to serve this important function.

Initial Presentations: The hard, fast sales pitch typical of an initial presentation should be avoided when dealing with the Japanese; rather than learning about your product, company, or service, the Japanese want first to learn about you and the members of your team. A slow, patient, sensitive presentation complete with printed handouts and copies of visual materials for each Japanese member to peruse later is important; high-pressured persuasion will not work but will only serve to intimidate the Japanese and make them distrustful of you and your company.

Japanese Behavior at Meetings: At meetings, Japanese behavior can be rather disconcerting to Americans unfamiliar with it; long stretches of silence, stone-faced stares, even a team member occasionally dozing off; then perhaps incessant talking and questioning, asking for information that was previously covered in great detail or for data that is inappropriate at the moment or of a classified nature. The Japanese negotiating team is extremely group-minded and will confer among themselves or remain deliberately vague and noncommittal until they have had a chance to do so. A typical reaction from Americans leaving such meetings is that the Japanese did not understand a word that was said or were being pointedly devious and uncommunicative.

Job Titles: In the status-conscious society from which the Japanese businessman comes, titles are extremely important; in fact, they may be more important than the actual responsibility they imply. Business cards should include your job title and be handed over early when meeting Japanese business people so they can assess the respect and deference due your position.

Lawyers: The Japanese have strong contempt for litigation as Westerners know it and prefer to exclude lawyers from most negotiating sessions; coming from a culture much less litigious than our own, they are distrustful of American business people who rely too heavily on legal advice when negotiating business ventures.

Letters of Understanding: Since negotiations can drag on over weeks or months and the Japanese prefer oral to written communication, it is a good idea to initiate letters of understanding occasionally when major breakthroughs have been achieved, stating your understanding of the terms agreed upon to that point and thus letting the Japanese have a chance to react to your interpretation; letters should be transmitted outside the formal negotiation session, preferably by the go-between.

Translators: As a rule, Americans are not comfortable dealing through translators and need to learn the general code of conduct to make the interpreter's task as easy as possible. Westerners usually rely on the Japanese to provide the translator, but two interpreters, one on each side, are better for everyone's sake.

Ultimatums: Exchanging ultimatums with the Japanese involves highly inflated language on both sides: They will give the impression they are being magnanimous about their position and that yours is unrealistic; such rhetoric is considered by them as necessary ritual and Americans should not be thrown off guard; ultimately, the Japanese will concede and compromise but only in the context of saving face and wording their concession so as to make their position look heroic. Do not suggest counterconcessions for them while making your own; the Japanese prefer to think they are coming up with their own proposals.

Written Contracts: Much business is conducted in Japan without written contracts; statements of agreement are more frequent and do not have the legal binding clauses that Westerners prefer. It is not uncommon for the Japanese to ask to renegotiate points that have been decided and written into contracts; in their view, good faith demands that all parties be willing to sit down and renegotiate if disagreements arise.

NOTES

Chapter 1

1. "Japan–U.S. Trade Friction," *Journal of Japanese Trade and Industry*, May 17, 1982, p. 5.
2. Martyn Naylor, "The Logic Gap," *Business in Japan*, ed. Paul Norbury and Geoffrey Bownas (Boulder, Colo.: Westview, 1980), p. 2.

Chapter 2

1. *Look Japan*, October 10, 1981, p. 26.
2. Potomac Associates, "The U.S. and Japan: American Perceptions and Policies," 1982.
3. Murrow Reports, "The American Press and Japan," Rodney Armstrong, 1979, pp. 6–9.
4. "Playboy Interview: Akio Morita," *Playboy*, August 1982, p. 77.
5. *Japan-America Dialogue* (New York: United States-Japan Foundation, 1981), pp. 23–24.
6. *Mainichi Daily News*, January 24, 1978.
7. Murrow Reports, "A Study: Japan's International Communication," October 1979, p. 10.
8. *Playboy*, August 1982, p. 84.
9. "Playboy Interview: Akio Morita," *Playboy*, August 1982, p. 80.
10. Jiro Tokuyama, "Hiding from Heaven and Earth," *Newsweek*, December 19, 1977, p. 34.
11. *Japan Times*, March 27, 1977, p. 8.
12. "Playboy Interview: Akio Morita," *Playboy*, August 1982, p. 82.
13. Jack Seward, *The Japanese* (New York: William Morrow & Co., 1972), p. 35.

14. Bruce Cummings, "The Conjurings of Japan," *Nation*, February 13, 1982, p. 188.
15. Murrow Reports, "A Study," p. 118.
16. *Mainichi Daily News*, January 31, 1978.
17. "Playboy Interview: Akio Morita," *Playboy*, August 1982, p. 77.
18. Seward, *The Japanese*, p. 29.
19. *New York Times*, August 6, 1982.
20. *Newsweek*, December 19, 1977, p. 34.
21. Richard Casement, "The Innovative Japanese," *Economist*, June 19, 1982, pp. 8–9.
22. William H. Forbis, *Japan Today: People, Places, Power* (New York: Harper and Row, 1975), p. 5.
23. *Ibid.*, p. 21.
24. *Economist*, June 19, 1982, p. 9.
25. *Ibid.*, p. 21.
26. Frank Gibney, *Japan: The Fragile Superpower* (New York: Charles E. Tuttle, 1975), p. 182.
27. *Mainichi Daily News*, February 14, 1978.
28. Potomac Associates, "American Attitudes Toward Japan," p. 3.
29. Yoshi Tsurumi, *The Japanese Are Coming: A Multinational Interaction of Firms and Politics* (Cambridge, Mass.: Ballinger Publishing Company, 1976), p. 303.
30. Murrow Reports, "A Study," p. 6.
31. *New York Times*, August 6, 1982.

Chapter 3

1. Hugh D. Menzies, "Can the Twain Meet at Mitsubishi?" *Fortune*, January 26, 1981, p. 43.
2. The Verbatim Record of "Electronics Industries Association of Japan" Seminar, "Management, Productivity and Reindustrialization, East Meets West," Washington, D.C., April 2, 1981, p. 27.
3. *New York Times*, January 7, 1983.
4. Talk given by Ray Gates, President of Panasonic Corporation at Columbia University Lecture Series, April 1982.
5. Richard T. Johnson, "Success and Failure of Japanese Subsidiaries in America," *Columbia Journal of World Business*, Spring 1977, p. 33.
6. *Ibid.*, p. 36.

7. Peter Drucker, "What We Can Learn from Japanese Management," *Harvard Business Review*, March-April 1971, p. 115.
8. "East Meets West" seminar, p. 33.
9. Peter Drucker, *Harvard Business Review*, March-April, 1971, p. 116.
10. *National Productivity Review*, 1981–82, p. 66.
11. Bruce Cummings, "The Conjurings of Japan," *Nation*, February 13, 1982, p. 181.
12. *Wall Street Journal,* January 26, 1981.
13. Alexander K. Young, *The Sogo Shosha: Japanese Multinational Trading Companies* (Boulder, Colo.: Westview, 1979), p. 22.
14. *Ibid.*, p. 3.
15. Yoshi Tsurumi, *The Japanese Are Coming: A Multinational Interaction of Firms and Politics* (Cambridge, Mass.: Ballinger Publishing Company, 1976), p. 236.
16. *New York Times,* April 18, 1982.
17. *Ibid.*
18. *New York Times*, November 21, 1982.
19. *New York Times*, February 23, 1982.
20. Hugh D. Menzies, "Can the Twain Meet at Mitsubishi?" *Fortune*, January 26, 1981, p. 43.
21. Richard T. Johnson, "Success and Failure of Japanese Subsidiaries in America," *Columbia Journal of World Business*, Spring 1977, p. 35.
22. Allan Dodds Frank, "The U.S. Side of the Street," *Fortune*, July 19, 1982, p. 31.

Chapter 4

1. Jack Seward, *Japanese in Action: Useful and Amusing Language Book* (Salem, Mass.: Weatherhill, 1969), p. 44.
2. Jack Seward, *The Japanese* (New York: William Morrow & Co., 1972), p. 257.

Chapter 5

1. Herb Cohen, *You Can Negotiate Anything* (Secaucus, N.J.: Lyle Stuart, 1980), p. 95.
2. Michael Blaker, *Japanese International Negotiating Style* (New York: Columbia University Press, 1977), p. 175.
3. "Playboy Interview: Akio Morita," *Playboy*, August 1982, p. 84.

Chapter 6

1. "Playboy Interview: Akio Morita," *Playboy*, August 1982, p. 80.
2. Japan Society, "The Economic Impact of the Japanese Business Community in the United States," 1979, p. 1.
3. This statement was made at the Conference Board Seminar entitled "Japanese Management of American Workforces," New York, April 20, 1982.
4. Hugh D. Menzies, "Can the Twain Meet at Mitsubishi?", *Fortune*, January 26, 1981, p. 44.
5. *Ibid.*
6. *Peace, Happiness, Prosperity* (International Edition: *A Forum for a Better World*), March 1983, pp. 14–15.
7. *The Executive Female*, March/April 1981, p. 35.

Chapter 7

1. *Advertising Age*, March 28, 1983, p. 23.
2. Japan Society, "Comparative Industries: Japan and the U.S. in the 1980s," March 1980, p. 13.
3. Masaaki Aoki and Satoshi Yoshida, "Bitter Experience Will Conquer the Barrier," *Journal of Japanese Trade and Industry*, May 1982, p. 52.
4. For a more complete analysis of these and other companies, see Gene Gregory, "Working with Japan's Free Market Structure," in *Business in Japan,* ed. Paul Norbury and Geoffrey Bownas (Boulder, Colo.: Westview, 1980), pp. 29–39.
5. See Robert Ballon, "Management Style," in *ibid.*, p. 119.
6. JETRO, *Facts and Finds Series No. 1*, "Keys to Success in the Japanese Market," 1980, p. 27.
7. *Ibid.*, p. 26.
8. For more on Japanese bank services, see Kunihiko Kobayashi and Takashi Sugiyama, "Services of a Japanese Bank," in *Business in Japan*, pp. 98–102.
9. JETRO REPORT 1980, p. 17. (See #6 above.)
10. Andrew Watt, "The Value of Market Research," in *Business in Japan*, p. 63.
11. JETRO REPORT 1980, p. 26. (See #6 above.)
12. The above is drawn from Watt, "The Value of Market Research," in *Business in Japan*, pp. 63–67.

13. David Gribbin, "The Role and Application of Advertising," in *Business in Japan*, p. 70. See this comprehensive study in its entirety, pp. 68–76.
14. JETRO REPORT 1980, p. 13. (See #6 above.)
15. MIPRO REPORT, No. 2, "Penetrating the Japanese Market," p. 10.
16. JETRO REPORT 1980, p. 7. (See #6 above.)
17. *Ibid.*, p. 9.
18. *Ibid.*
19. See Masao Okamoto, "Rationalizing the Distribution System," in *Business in Japan*, pp. 57–63.
20. *Ibid.*
21. *Ibid.*
22. Some of the material in this subsection is adapted from Mitsuaki Shimaguchi and Larry J. Rosenberg, "Demystifying Japanese Distribution," *Columbia Journal of World Business*, Spring 1979, pp. 32–41.
23. JETRO REPORT 1980, p. 11. (See #6 above.)
24. JETRO REPORT 1980, pp. 26–27. (See #6 above.)